Black Pupils Matter

OUR EXPERIENCE OF THE ENGLISH EDUCATION SYSTEM
1950 – 2000

Wasuk Godwin Sule-Pearce

First published in the United Kingdom in 2022 by
The Choir Press
ISBN 978-1-78963-276-7

Cover design and layout by Stuart Blackburn Publicity

Wasuk Godwin Sule-Pearce

This book examines the English curriculum and teacher pedagogical approach with a comprehensive look at its effects on Black students. Based on an ethnographic research approach, *Black Pupils Matter: Our Experiences of the English Education System 1950-2000* consists of stories of then students who are now either parents or educators of Black students.

Black Africans and Caribbeans in the 1970s had high educational expectations and a successful career and a prosperous future for their children: something that has not materialised to this day. Unfortunately, the cycle has continued from first generation Black immigrants who feel that they failed at school to generations X, Y and Z, who continue to perform below national average expected levels. The focus of this book is to elevate the voices of Black people and to propose a *global curriculum and culturally relevant pedagogical approach* which would ensure representation and equitable outcomes for Black people in education.

In this book I offer an insight into the English education system through research, and the lens of narrative enquiry and analysis. Research on Black students over the past decade has focused on the attainment gap, exclusion rates, and race and racism in education. Improving the Black student experience in education is not straight forward. Educators and policy makers are highly resistant to change but through such research we expect to find further clarification of what strategies work for Black students and why these strategies are effective in improving the Black student schooling experience.

Suitable for scholars and researchers in education, parents, students and practitioners on the front lines, *Black Pupils Matter: Our Experience of the English Education System 1950-2000* will spur on a debate on best practices for interrupting the vicious cycle of experiences for Black people in the English education system.

Wasuk Godwin Sule-Pearce is a doctoral candidate at the University of West London currently undertaking a three-year transnational research project that explores the lived experiences of Black lesbian, gay, bisexual, transgender and queer+ students in Higher Education Institutes in the United Kingdom, North America and South Africa. She was born and educated in Uganda and while in the United Kingdom obtained a Masters degree in Accountancy and a Masters degree in Applied Project Management. She is a mother of four wonderful children with the eldest at university and the other three being home schooled.

Wasuk is the author of a series of Key Stage 2, The Geography of Africa Study and Activity books and is currently working on a similar format for Key Stage 2, The History of Africa books. Details are listed on page 121.

For more information about these books, please visit:
https://wasukp.com/

Dedication

To all those who accepted my call and generously shared their stories in this research, and to my family who taught me perseverance, genuine kindness, and love.

Acknowledgments

This book would not have been possible without the generous support of others. First, I would like to thank the participants who shared their stories in this project. I am deeply humbled and honoured to have met you, talked with you and become a part of your story. I hope I have represented your voices well and am forever grateful for your gift of openness, vulnerability and time.

To my family and friends, I am incredibly thankful for your guidance and encouragement. My husband, Kieron Pearce, who is the most loving human being I have met, ready to cook, counsel and care. Thank you for believing in me. My children Liam, Xavier, Gloria and Violette, you inspire me to do better every day and I love you so very much. To John Root, thank you for reading every dot, space, comma and line.

Finally, thank you to the wonderful Associate Professor Yu-Chun Pan. Your supervision and support have been pivotal in my academic success and career. To Professor William Lez Henry, thank you for generously giving of your time. It is thanks to your advice that I wrote this book.

Key Quotes

‘This was the 80s. There was racism, you had to fight that and try and get an education at the same time’ **Douglas**

‘My academics suffered and I missed out. Your school days are supposed to be the happiest. But when that is not right, the foundation is weak and the future is bleak’ **Dorothy**

‘Teachers control the school space and they will determine your outcome, so I tell Black parents to prepare their children so they know when to challenge teachers and when not to. Brief your children and debrief them as you are sending them in an enemy environment’ **Dylan**

‘Children have to be at the centre of recruitment and why we get into teaching and not the other way around. I remember my personal statement, when I wanted to become a teacher, made the panel cry because there was so much love and passion in there. In every job I have done, the young person continues to be at the centre. Sorry, if a teacher does not have that, no unconscious bias training is going to correct this. I am very suspicious. I have seen teachers who love their subject but do not love the children’ **Doris**

‘When I had problems with my maths teacher, I approached another teacher who was Black. I remember talking to him about my experiences in the classroom and my mum talked to him as well. The Black teacher supported me and would explain things I had not understood in the lesson. Thanks for his help I did well in maths. Schools should provide to the students and parents a list of teachers and timetable of when they are available to help. Teachers can make or break you’ **Dolores**

‘Growing up I hesitated getting involved in some things because I was not sure that it was my place’ **Delilah**

‘If you were Black, they would allow you in the top set but they constantly checked to make sure you could do the work. As opposed to the White pupils who they just left to get on with it. It was as though they did not trust that a Black pupil was good enough to be up there. We had to work twice as hard to prove that we had a place in that set. Constantly having to maintain your place is tiring’ **Delilah**

‘Slavery was taught in a light-hearted way. As I researched slavery, I realised that we were not taught about the discrimination and how slaves were transferred to other countries. Back then I did not think much of it but as I grew older, I started to wonder whether this was really the history of my culture or the English perspective’ **Dale**

'The relationship was purely teacher-pupil and nothing like where we could have a chat. It was always about the school work and no interest in me at all. This sort of a relationship limited my ability because all they were interested in were my grades but I did not really matter. It was demotivating' **Dale**

'I was nowhere in the subjects I was taught. The boys in the books were blond, blue eyed. How could I find any interest in only reading books that had White people in them? I hated the slavery lesson. I could feel all those White kids looking at me. In fact, I remember the kids saying I looked like some of the kids we had seen in the lesson. It was horrifying. We do not include Black people and when we do, it is in a derogatory way' **Dean**

'I think the teacher relationship affected me the most. If all my teachers had been like my P.E. teacher then maybe I could be a teacher now' **Derek**

'The expectations set for me in primary school were low and I proved them wrong. It was the same for secondary school. I think expectations were set based on race for Black pupils and class for some White pupils. So regardless of your class as a Black pupil, the expectations were the same as a lower-class White pupil. This made me work harder. I do not know what the solution is' **Delilah**

'Back then I thought sets were determined on your results but I know they are determined on behaviour' **Dale**

'When I look at my son's work, I do not think that what is covered today during Black history month is sufficient. They talk briefly about Black historical figures like Rosa Parks and Nelson Mandela, but I think there is more to African and Caribbean culture that should be included. They just do this to cover their backs and say I have taught Black history but ethically they have not' **Darcy**

'Another area is the lack of Black books which really hurts Black kids. This causes them to lose themselves and their self-esteem because they are around a culture that tells them that Black is worthless and has not contributed to the country' **Darcy**

'Had they introduced more of the Black culture way of living, a lot of false information would have been erased. Maybe we could all have understood that we are equal' **Debra**

'I think teachers think that all Black people are capable of is playing football and singing. There was a lot of Black kids in these activities. I think this is also the case today. When you look at football or the music industry' **Derek**

Contents

Chapter 1: Introduction

Background and Significance

What is education?

If you were to ask anyone what education is, the answers would most likely vary from it helps me learn, to getting a job, with some defining education based on their lived experiences of the schooling system. Therefore, it is difficult to pinpoint exactly what education is. There have been attempts to define education since the philosophers Socrates and Plato. However, Mathew and Wells (1999) argue that we are nowhere near reaching one that is agreeable. According to Gregory (2002), education equips minds to make sense of the physical, social and cultural world. However, some such as Peters (1966), have suggested that the term education implies that there is an intent to transmit in a morally acceptable way, something that is considered worthwhile. This leads us to ask, what is an intent to transmit? What is morally acceptable? Who sets the standards?

The term education is further complicated because some associate it with schooling, learning and training and consider schooling synonymous with education. While some, such as Carr (2003) suggest that the relationship between learning and teaching is causal, Gregory (2002) argues they are distinct and the relationship cannot be assumed. To this extent some argue that these differences shape their understanding of education on leaving a schooling system that they sometimes believe has failed them. Something very few people doubt though is that there is a connection between education, social development and economic performance (Alexander, 2008).

In the context of this discussion, I will begin with education from the 15th century. In Europe children were taught by their parents or neighbours. In some cases older women in the village or town ran a small cranny school which combined childcare with teaching the children to recite bible verses or psalms (Wiesner-Hanks 2013). In France, some schools taught reading, writing, singing the liturgy and arithmetic: in parts of Italy, men taught middle and working-class boys reading, writing, bookkeeping and accounting in abbaco schools: in parts of Spain, priests and sacristans taught reading and writing and fathers sent at least one son to school. One went to school based on one's class, religion, gender and geographic location, among other factors.

In the 16th century, Protestant reformers opened schools to teach children vernacular and proper religious values. According to Martin Luther, salvation depended on each person's own reading of the scriptures therefore each person had to learn to read and also learn

1

that the scriptures represented absolute truths and that salvation depended on understanding those truths. The Lutheran leaders of the Reformation promoted public education as a Christian duty, to save souls from hell. By 1580, in the province of Electoral Saxony in central Germany, 50% of the parishes had German-language school for boys and 10% for girls, Germany was considered best in class in Europe. In England, some dioceses had English-language elementary schools in about half of their parishes.

At the end of the 17th and into the 18th century, Methodist and Utilitarianism made up the dominant ideology and discipline of the Industrial Revolution. These beliefs were replicated in the Evangelical movement in all churches and the attitudes held about children in the Sunday schools promoted by the Church of England, was that they were not to be considered *innocent beings* but rather a *corrupt nature and evil disposition*. According to Thompson (1980), in the 1790s and 1800s, Sunday schools that were promoted by the Church of England fostered discipline and repression and it was reported that the function of the schools in Halifax and Stockport was to instil in the children of the poor *a spirit of industry, economy and piety*. Sunday school teachers were instructed to:

"Tame the ferocity of their unsubdued passion: to repress the excessive rudeness of their manner: to chasten the disgusting and demoralizing obscenity of their language: to subdue the stubborn rebellion of their wills: to render them honest, obedient, courteous, industrious, submissive and orderly" (Russell, 1960).

Children learned to read from the Bible, which included short rhymes to help them learn the alphabet, beginning with, *In **Adam's** Fall, We sinned all and ending with **Z**accheus he, Did climb the tree, His Lord to see.* The Bible also included the Lord's Prayer, the creed, the Ten Commandments, all designed to drill into the children a fear of God and a sense of duty to their elders.

Towards the end of the 17th century, 94% of the parishes in Electoral Saxony had German-language schools for boys and 40% for girls and schooling was made mandatory in most German states. The schools were run by the Lutheran church and separated by gender in most large towns but sometimes this was not possible in small towns (Wiesner-Hanks, 2013). Catholic Reformers also taught reading and writing to boys and girls in separate schools. Children were taught to read first and then write later because it was cheaper that way round. In the Ottoman empire, private or religious schools taught boys and sometimes girls to read, write and recite the Qur'an. Between 1450 and 1750, literacy numbers slowly increased with the highest numbers seen among the upper classes of northwest Europe and lowest among the rural peasantry of south and east Europe. By 1750, almost all upper-class men and women could read, unlike the peasants. In most cities in Europe men were twice as likely able to be able to sign a parish register, marriage contract or a will and in the cases women signed, their signature was poorly written as according to Wiesner-hanks (2013) their name was the only thing they could write.

During the middle-ages, schools were controlled by churches but by mid-15th and all through the 16th century, rulers and city governments took over schools and academies, deciding on the curriculum. Once a Christian boy had learned to read and write in the vernacular, or before that if he was from a wealthy family, they were sent to a Latin grammar school or college. Protestants supported the Latin grammar schools and it was estimated that there were 400 such schools in England. In the 16th century, in Catholic countries such as Spain, France and Poland, members of the Reformed church staffed the grammar schools and colleges in order to shape education. And by mid-16th century, they ran thirty-three colleges in seven European countries. Latin grammar schools were only open to Christians and they trained clergy and laymen. In the Ottoman Empire and the rest of the Muslim world, colleges madrasas trained legal scholars in Islamic law and tradition (Wiesner-Hanks, 2013).

By the 16th century there were over fifty universities in Europe and, in the Christian parts, universities offered the highest level of education. Italian universities including Padua and Bologna focused on law and medicine and they attracted young men from all over Europe who had already mastered Latin in an academy or college. Students at Paris and Oxford universities studied for a bachelor's degree and, their teachers had a master's degree. Paris and Salamanca were the largest universities in Europe. The existence of universities in Europe was threatened by Protestant and Catholic Reformer wars when the secular authorities with jurisdiction started to demand an oath of religious orthodoxy from students and teachers. This was the case for Pope Pius IV in 1564 and Elizabeth I in 1580 where they demanded allegiance to Catholicism and Protestantism respectively, or else students and teachers alike were dismissed and, in some cases, executed. Therefore, by 1600, scholarly contact, mobility and exchange was difficult because of religious differences (Wiesner-Hanks, 2013).

What is the meaning of curriculum?
The word curriculum has been defined as a set of the body of knowledge, skills and understanding that a community wishes to hand over to the next generation of its young people (Parliament, 2009), or a social fact that is not only restricted to subjects taught but justifies why the curriculum is appropriate and what effect it will have on the recipients

(Young, 2014). I define curriculum as the knowledge and cultural norms that are cultivated into the next generation. A national curriculum is a set of subjects and standards used by schools to ensure that pupils learn the same thing. It introduces pupils to the best that has been thought and said and helps engender an appreciation of human creativity and achievement (DfE 2014). Once again, the questions should be: The best that has been thought and said by whom? Who sets the standards?

Curriculum in 15th and 17th century Europe, was organised around reading, writing, arithmetic, languages, religious education, hymn-singing, worship services, sewing and embroidery in schools: book keeping and accounting, Greek natural philosophy, modern foreign languages and doctrine in colleges: and universities offered law, medicine and anatomy and Latin, Greek and Hebrew language (Wiesner-Hank, 2013). Today, the national curriculum in England is organised into blocks of years called key stages (KS) (Roberts, 2021). At the end of each KS, the teacher will formally assess pupils' performance in the different subjects (see Table 1)

	Early Years Foundation Stage (EYFS)	KS1	KS2	KS3	KS4
AGE	4-5	5-7	7-11	11-14	14-16
YEAR GROUPS	0	1-2	3-6	7-9	10-11
CORE SUBJECTS					
ENGLISH / LITERACY	X	X	X	X	X
MATHEMATICS	X	X	X	X	X
SCIENCE		X	X	X	X
FOUNDATION SUBJECTS					
ART & DESIGN / EXPRESSIVE ART & DESIGN (EAD)	X	X	X	X	
CITIZENSHIP				X	X
COMPUTING		X	X	X	X
DESIGN & TECHNOLOGY		X	X	X	
LANGUAGES / COMMUNICATION & LANGUAGE (CAL)	X		X	X	
GEOGRAPHY		X	X	X	
HISTORY		X	X	X	
MUSIC		X	X	X	
PHYSICAL EDUCATION / PHYSICAL DEVELOPMENT (PD)	X	X	X	X	X
RELIGIOUS EDUCATION		X	X	X	X
RELATIONSHIP & SEX EDUCATION				X	X
PERSONAL, SOCIAL, & EMOTIONAL DEVELOPMENT (PSED)	X				
UNDERSTANDING THE WORLD (UTW)	X				

Table 1
Structure of the national curriculum in England

During the Middle Ages, secondary and higher education was, for the majority of the time, controlled by the church, but by mid-15th century, rulers and city governments had begun to support secular schools and academies. This system continued well into the 16th century, with cities hiring and licensing schoolmasters and determining the curriculum. Today, the Secretary of State for Education sets the curriculum, which outlines the content and matters to be taught in the subjects at the relevant Key Stages. Since 1944, there have been different laws enacted by parliament that have impacted the curriculum, schooling and education of children and young adults (DfE, 2014) (see Table 2)

Year	Act/ Government	Action
1944	Education Act	It raised school leaving age to 15 and made secondary school education free for all.
1952	Children and Young Persons (Amendment) Act	It was to protect children in care.
1953	Education Act	It required local authorities to provide education and care for pupils at educational institutes maintained by them.
1958	Matrimonial Proceedings (Children) Act 1958	This was to protect the interests of children in divorce cases
1959	Mental Health Act	This was to ensure that mentally ill patients benefited from health and social service facilities.
1962	Education Act	It required all local authorities to give grants to qualifying students from their area to enrol on qualifying courses anywhere in the UK.
1970	Education (free School Milk) Act	It extended the provision of free milk to pupils in middle school.
1970	Education (Handicapped Children) Act	Discontinued the classification of disabled children as unfit for education at school.
1971	Education (Milk) Act	Abolished the provision of free school milk for 8-to 11-year-olds.
1975	Child Benefit Act	It replaced family allowances with child benefit.
1976	Education School Leaving Act	It made provision for school leaving age.
1976	Race Relations Act	It updated laws on racial discrimination and established the Commission for Racial Equality.
1979	Education Act	It allowed local education authorities to retain selective secondary schools.
1980	Education Act	Parents were given rights to choose their children's schools.

Table 2 *continued overleaf*
Acts of Parliament relating to children and young adults;
schools and education in England, 1944 -2021

1981	Education Act	It required that children previously referred to as 'handicapped' were instead to be termed *pupils with special educational needs* (SEN) and a written statement of those needs was to be made for each child and there was increased emphasis on integrated provision in their education.
1986	Education (No. 2) Act	It prohibited corporal punishment in all schools receiving state funding.
1988	Education Reform Act	It introduced the National Curriculum, SATs Tests, GCSEs, league tables, more parental choice and the establishment of an 'education market place' which was driven by competition, diversity and choice.
1990	Education (Student Loans) Act	It introduced 'top-up' loans for higher education students and so began the disappearance of student grants.
1992	Further and Higher Education Act	It removed more than 500 further education and sixth form colleges from local education authority (LEA) control and established Further Education Funding Councils (FEFCs). It allowed polytechnics to apply for university status, unified the funding of higher education under the Higher Education Funding Councils (HEFCs), introduced competition for funding between institutions and abolished the Council for National Academic Awards (CNAA).
1993	Education Act	It made it easier for schools to become grant-maintained, it laid down rules for pupil exclusions and for 'failing' schools, it replaced the National Curriculum Council (NCC) and the School Examinations and Assessment Council (SEAC) with the School Curriculum and Assessment Authority (SCAA) and defined SEN.
1996	Education (Student Loan) Act	It advanced public sector student loans to the private sectors.
1996	Nursery Education and Grant Maintained Schools Act	Provided grants for nursery education and permitted borrowing for grant-maintained schools.
1996	Education Act	It required the Education Authority (EA), formerly the Education and Library Boards (ELBs), to identify, assess and make provision for children with SEN within their area.
1997	Education Act	It extended the assisted places scheme to primary schools, laid down new rules for the restraint, detention and exclusion of pupils and replaced the National Council for Vocational Qualifications (NCVQ) and the School Curriculum and Assessment Authority (SCAA) with the Qualifications and Curriculum Authority (QCA).
1997	Education Act	It abolished the assisted places scheme.
1998	School Standards and Framework Act	It encouraged selection by specialisation, changed the names of types of schools, limited infant class sizes and established Education Action Zones.

Year	Act	Description
1999	The Protection of Children Act	It provided for a list to be kept of people considered unsuitable to work with children and those suffering from mental impairment.
2000	Care Standards Act	It established the National Care Standards Commission, the General Social Care Council and the Care Council.
2001	Special Education Needs and Disability Act	It made further provision against discrimination on grounds of disability in schools and in further and higher education institutions.
2004	Higher Education Act	It established the Arts and Humanities Research Council and appointed the Director of Fair Access to Higher Education: it set out arrangements for dealing with students' complaints about higher education institutions: made provisions relating to grants and loans to students in higher and further education.
2006	Equality Act	It established the Commission for Equality and Human Rights with implications for schools.
2008	Sale of Student Loans Act	It allowed the government to sell student loans to private companies.
2008	Special Education Needs (Information) Act	It made provision for the publication of information about children with special educational needs.
2008	Education and Skills Act	It replaced the school leaving age of 16 with an education leaving age of 18 and made a variety of provisions relating to the education or training of young adults.
2009	Apprenticeship, Skill, Children and Learning Act	It created a framework for apprenticeships and established the Young People's Learning Agency for England (YPLA), the office of Chief Executive of Skills Funding, the Office of Qualifications and Examinations Regulation (Ofqual) and the School Support Staff Negotiating Body (SSSNB).
2010	Child Poverty Act	This set targets relating to the eradication of child poverty and provided for the establishment of the Child Poverty Commission.
2010	Equality Act	Stated that schools could not unlawfully discriminate against pupils because of their sex, race, disability, religion or belief or sexual orientation.
2011	Education Act	Introduced legal power for teachers to root out poor behaviour, tackle underperformance and ways to hold schools accountable and abandoned the upper age limit of 18 for participation in education.
2014	Children & Families Act	It was designed to protect vulnerable children, parents and families.
2017	Children & Social Work Act	It was established to improve the welfare of looked after children.
2017	Higher Education & Research Act	It was established to support the government's mission to boost social mobility, life chances and opportunity for all.
2019	Relationship Education, Relationship and Sex Education (RSE) and Health Education	It is guidance for schools on their legal duties when teaching Relationships Education, Relationship and Sex Education (RSE) and Health Education.

What is the meaning of pedagogy?

Pedagogy is a term derived from French and Latin versions of Greek *paidos* for boy plus *agogos* for *leader*. Precisely, meaning a man leading a boy to school (Knowles 1980). It is an intentional act by one person intended to enhance learning in another (Mortimore 1999): or teaching someone what they need to know and the skills they need to command in order to make and justify the many different kinds of decisions of which teaching is constituted (Alexander 2008: DfES 2007b): or the way in which teachers rethink the space of learning and how they rearrange the classroom to manage the exclusion of marginalised communities and understanding the complementary relationship between teaching and learning (Corries, 2014).

Teaching is not entirely about transmitting knowledge but to enable the learner to generate and evaluate knowledge while the teacher continues to provide information and alternative sources. Pupils are looked at as thinkers who share knowledge with the teacher. However, some have argued that *what is learned relates strongly to the situation in which it is learnt* (Brown et al., 1989) and, unless learners understand the differences in contexts, knowledge obtained in one is not transferable (Cox 1997). 21st century research has shown that there is a correlation between success and how a teacher handles the complexities in a classroom and wider context including: age, syllabus, stage of learner and purpose of learning (Moretimore 1999). Teaching and learning can be reciprocal.

Another aspect of teaching relates to teaching styles. In post-World War II Europe, studies characterised the act of teaching as either authoritarian or democratic or a laissez faire style (Lewin et al., 1939) or integrative or dominative (Anderson 1946). Studies in the 80s found that traditional (authoritarian and dominative) styles of teaching were predominant in the primary schools in the United Kingdom (UK) (Alexander 1995). This greatly impacts the act of talk and, as found by Alexander (2008), of all the tools available for cultural and pedagogical intervention in human development, talk is the most far reaching in its use and powerful in its possibilities. Talk is a mediator of psychological and cultural spaces between teacher-pupil, pupil-pupil and, society-individual. What is more, talk facilitates what the pupil currently knows and understands and what they are to know and understand in the future. Language structures thinking and speech shapes the higher mental processes that are necessary for learning to take place. However, talk that engages pupils and fosters their understanding is rare in UK classrooms because teachers rather than pupils control the talking, what is said, who says it and to whom.

According to Tharp and Gallimore (1988), pupils practice the *recitation script* of closed teacher questions, brief recall answers and minimal feedback that requires them to report someone else's thinking, rather than think for themselves and they are assessed on their accuracy or compliance in doing so. And, in an attempt to avoid authoritarianism, teachers ask open ended questions that are unfocussed and unchallenging and give emphatic praise rather than meaningful feedback. One-sided talk is detrimental to a pupil's ability to learn quickly and effectively: it might affect the development of a pupil's narration, explanatory and questioning powers, ultimately affecting their ability to challenge what they are being taught: and it may ill-inform teachers about a pupil's current knowledge and understanding, leading to difficulties in assessment (Tharp and Gallimore, 1988).

It is crucial to note, that in order for pedagogy as defined above to apply to all, teachers must note that our societies are largely diverse and continuously changing due to vast expansion of communications, information technology and artificial intelligence. Pedagogy must adapt to keep up with these developments and seek to engage and support all learners to generate knowledge and manage change. Just as teachers have had to adjust their teaching styles since the industrial revolution, as well as obtain managerial and organisational skills to handle the complexities of a classroom (Arends 1994), they are required to respond to the increasing social, economic, technological, environmental and political changes (Watkins, 1997).

As far as Black pupils are concerned, a critical Black pedagogy must, in Freire's words understand and empathise with a Black person's lived experiences. Knowledge should be co-created, by the teacher and pupils learning from each other. Freire (2017) urges for basic dialogue where the teachers have humility and faith in pupils and for pupils to have the ability to review processes critically and reject inappropriate views. Furthermore, the content and syllabus taught should consist of organised information that represents the things that Black pupils would like to learn more about. In the case that this is difficult to achieve, then Black pupils should be fully supported to identify the problems and solutions and only then can they be the masters of their thinking. Illich (1971) urges for the reconstruction of a critical pedagogy of technology that is capable of speaking to today's needs and the current terrain in education. Technology can boost learning and knowledge and become a vehicle used to overcome inequalities through the appropriate establishment of critical consciousness on the issues surrounding culture and society.

Statement of the Problem

In the 1940s, Black Caribbean people were recruited to come work in England. Similar to the Black immigrants from other regions that had come before them, the Black Caribbean parents expected their children to have a much more enhanced education automatically followed by opportunities and a prosperous future. Unfortunately, Black pupils have not shared in the higher education standards attained by the most successful pupils in schools in England, HMI (2002). Furthermore, Black pupils have reportedly continued to perform below the national average expected levels, DfE (2017). Many Black parents that attended school in the 60s and 70s feel they failed at school and are determined that the cycle will not repeat itself with their children and grandchildren, HMI (2002).

Previous studies have found that attainment is linked to numerous factors. Haynes et al. (2006) identified social factors: for Blanden & Gregg (2004), it was the impact of family income: Cooper & Stewart (2013) explored how economic factors affect children's outcomes: Chowdry et al. (2013) suggested that academic performance was linked to levels of a parents' education: and Letourneau et al. (2011) examined the impact of a parents, occupation on child development and educational attainment. Today, the attainment gap has been linked to all the above and special education needs and disability. According to the Education Endowment Foundation (2018), educational inequalities start in very early childhood and the effects continue throughout a person's life, impacting their entry into higher education, future employment and lifetime earnings (Pillas et al., 2014: OECD 2018). The COVID-19 pandemic has led to increased educational inequalities and attainment gaps in the short, medium and long-term (Education Endowment Foundation, 2021).

Aim and Objectives

The aim of this study is to investigate how the curriculum and pedagogy impacted the academic performance of Black pupils in the English education system between the year 1950 and 2000. The following research questions guided the study:

1. How did the national curriculum in England impact the academic performance of Black pupils?

2. How did the teacher pedagogical approach impact the academic performance of Black pupils in England?

Scope of the Study

At the design stage of this study, the focus was very much on how both the English national curriculum and teacher pedagogical approach impacted the academic performance of Black pupils rather than the ethnicity of their teachers. However, as I stated in the methodology section, research has shown that schools are staffed by majority White middle-class women and it is likely that the majority of participants were taught by White teachers. As such, this study was limited in understanding the impact of White teachers in the academic performance of Black pupils. Not to mention, the possibility that the national curriculum is designed by an all-White team. This merits a study of its own in order to fully address the impact of a Eurocentric curriculum on Black pupils. Never the less I focused on Black participants. As a qualitative study, it was not my intention to have results that are statistically generalisable, though patterns and processes may be transferable. I acknowledge the risk of treating Black pupils as a monolithic group and suggest that a narrative inquiry approach would help minimise generalisations and stereotypes, by taking a holistic view of their experiences.

Chapter one of this book is the introduction which you are engaged with at present. It features, a background to education, the definition of the English national curriculum and pedagogy. In addition, it details the aims and objectives of this study along with a statement of the problem, the scope and definition of terms. Chapter two details the methodology including the research paradigm, instrument, data collection and analysis, limitations of the study and ethical considerations. Chapter three explores the participants' narrative accounts and finally in chapter four, I discuss the stories and compare the data to literature. I also state the implications for the Department for Education (DfE), local authorities, educators and administrators and parents. In addition, I highlight lessons learnt and conclude.

Definition of Terms

The following list sets out a common understanding of the terms used in this study.

Black. A person that self-identifies as Black and are of Sub-Sharan African ancestry.

Credibility. is the extent to which the findings can be trusted and considered credible research.

Curriculum. Knowledge and cultural norms that are cultivated into the next generation.

Dependability. Consistency between data and results.

Expectations. Attitudes held about pupils to reach their potential.

National Curriculum. Set of subjects and standards used by schools to ensure that pupils learn the same thing.

Narrative. A way of telling and knowing about human life experiences. Narratives make up a story. In narrative therapy, narrative, in essence, is a metaphor for life experiences.

Narrative Coherence. How much the narratives make sense in context and the overall, unity of the story. Qualitative researchers seek coherence in their data, though narrative inquirers embrace unsuccessful efforts toward coherence.

Narrative Inquiry. A methodology that explores a storyteller's narratives of their life experiences.

Pedagogy. Intentional act by one person intended to enhance learning in another.

Place. One of three common places of narrative inquiry that focuses on how people and stories are intimately related and located in a particular place.

Polyphony. Concept that invites and embraces multiple voices and interpretations to engage the multiplicities of identity and life experiences.

Representation. Process by which meaning is produced and exchanged between members of a culture through the use of language, signs and images which stand for or represent things.

Shared narrative meaning. Common threads among the stories.

Story. Detailed organization of events, characters, context and plot that forms a fuller description of a person's life experiences. A story consists of narratives.

Threads. Echoes across data.

Transferability. Is a means by which we determine how relatable or transferable the findings are to the experiences of others who fit in the community we are interested in.

Urban pedagogical approach. A teaching style where the teacher makes references to popular culture and uses examples that pupils can connect with.

Chapter 2: Methodology

Narrative interviews are the stories lived and told by someone (Clandinin & Connelly, 2000). In this study, the participants are considered storytellers in the research process. These narrative interviews consist of semi-structured face to face interviews that were used to generate a fuller story of the nature of impact of the national curriculum and teacher pedagogical approach on the academic performance of Black pupils in England between the years 1950 and 2000. Narrative interview involves collecting stories, reporting personal experiences and ordering the meaning of those experiences (Creswell and Poth, 2018) while at the same time, describing the participant stories as both a method and the phenomenon of study (Pinnegar & Daynes, 2007). Qualitative researchers encourage participants to describe their experiences from their lens (Patton, 2002).

Research Paradigm

This study on the academic performance of Black pupils in England was based on four levels of developing a research study in mind (Saunders et al., 2016) (see Figure 1). I reorganised personal stories in a meaningful way as part of data analysis. Similar to this, Ollerenshaw & Creswell (2000) recommend that the story teller and researcher collect and analyse stories from a narrative perspective. The research design was compatible with the research paradigm so much that reality and stories were generated through the lived experiences and sharing process. As far back as 1500 BC, storytelling has been used as a tool for data collection and this form continues to evolve, making use of temporary sequences of lived experiences for a systematic and self-reflective search of the genuine self (Bamberg, 2010, p.6).

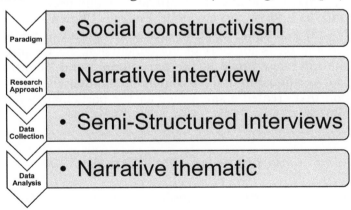

Figure 1
Four levels of research design

Research Instrument

In narrative research, the researcher collects information about the participant and formulates an understanding surrounding the participant's life. With the participant as the storyteller, the researcher is the audience that needs to reflect on the participant's personal and cultural background. As the researcher, I am responsible for the lens in which I view and tell the story and shape the way in which the story is told and generated (Creswell, 2013). Therefore, it is of the utmost importance that I recognise my position, identity and social context and since I cannot separate myself from my values, they inevitably influence the participants' narratives. My values also influence my data analysis process.

I can manage my bias by being transparent and accountable and I did this by including the participants in my analytical process during the interviews and I discussed what my thoughts were as I was listening to their experiences. This way participants could clear up any misunderstandings and note any inaccuracies and elaborate on how this departed from their understanding of their story. For instance, one participant considered being placed in an English as an additional language set as detrimental to their performance. Since my focus was on set placement based on attainment, I did not take the time to delve into set placement based on someone's immigration status and the participant was glad to describe in detail how this had impacted their experience.

The crucial part of the researcher-narrator relationship in narrative research is that it gives both the opportunity to learn and grow through the process (Pinnegar & Daynes, 2007). This was the case early on in the interviewing process when I realised that participants were highlighting the significance of the teaching methods they experienced and the impact this had on their performance. I therefore pondered the opportunity of having included both curriculum and pedagogy as areas explored and, as a follow up question, I asked, "Which had the most impact on your academic performance, curriculum or pedagogy?". This formed the basis for part of my conclusion. As we progressed through the interview process, the participants and I continued to negotiate our relationship and its transition throughout and it is this collaboration that created a safe space for the participant's narratives (Creswell, 2013).

Sampling and Recruitment

For eligibility, the participants needed to self-identify as Black and a pupil in England between the years 1950 and 2000 and, be aged 18 and above, which was likely given that data was collected in 2018. I appreciate that some Black people in England may choose to describe their racial identity differently (e.g., African, Black British, Afro-Caribbean, Afro-British). However, for this study, the term Black was used to refer to persons that self-identify as such and were of Sub-Saharan African ancestry. What is more, the letter B in Black, in this study, is spelt in upper case in order to empower Black people as opposed to and in defiance of, White cultural and political supremacy or a White-dominated society. In 1878 Ferdinand Lee Barnett championed the cause of capitalising the word Negro, as a fight against disrespect from the Whites. Similarly, in 1920, Marcus Garvey demanded that the word Negro be capitalised in order to preserve the dignity and self-respect of the New Negro who had been in the lower case for generations. Likewise, Chambers (2017) argues that when speaking of a culture, ethnicity or a group of people, Black should be capitalised. Furthermore, by referring to participants as pupils, I hoped to focus on primary and secondary school and this turned out to be the case with all participants. I recruited the participants primarily from the Black community and colleges in West London and this snowballed into recruiting from other areas including East, North and South East London. Participants were recruited through word of mouth, email, flyers, short message service and WhatsApp.

Data Collection

Participants were given the informed consent form in order to ensure they were eligible to participate and to describe the purpose of the study and their rights as participants. After completing the informed consent form, I emailed participants to set up their interview. Data collection was via semi-structured interviews conducted either face to face or over the telephone and they were approximately 45 minutes long. I recruited 23 participants, who were former pupils and some of whom were, at the time, parents or teachers and they, all but 1, self-identified as Black (see Table 3). According to Saunders et al. (2016), semi-structured interviews are a qualitative form of data collection that is defined by a pre-set question guide with an aim to provide in-depth results through storytelling. I chose semi-structured interviews because it was the intention of the study to answer the research questions by asking specific questions, but not so limited as to miss-out unanticipated information (structured) or so much as to generate irrelevant data (unstructured).

	Black	White	Total
Pupils	15		15
Teachers		1	1
Former pupil now parent or teacher	6		6
Total	21	1	22

Table 3
The characteristics and ethnicity of participants

Interview. At the start of the interview, I reminded the participants of their rights to ensure they were still happy to take part. If this was the case, I proceeded to gather stories about each participant's experiences at school including what they remembered being taught. This offered the participants a chance to mention the subjects, content and what sets they were in for each of the core subjects. We talked about expectations and got the participants to think about what expectations were set for them by their teachers and their parents.

I also asked the participants to recall their interactions with teachers, how they experienced these interactions and the impact this had on their academic performance. Furthermore, I investigated classroom sizes and seat arrangements, whether this was out of choice or a requirement by the teacher and how this impacted their academic performance. At the end of the interview, I checked to make sure the participants were well.

Data Transcript and Storage

I transcribed all interviews to prepare for analysis. The transcriptions were de-coded during transcription using the participant's pseudonym. After each transcript was completed, I double-checked it for accuracy and removed any identifying information. I used **Baby Name Voyager** to allocate names to participants. I decided that all participant names would start with letter D. If the interviewee was female, I typed letter D and selected from the list of popular names from the year they were born and likewise if it were a male interviewee.

Data Analysis

I analysed the data using the narrative thematic analysis (Riessman, 2008). I focused on what was told in the Black pupil's experience of the curriculum and pedagogy narratives and identified the various narrative thematic elements including: (a) place (b) event (c) characters (d) time and (e) plot (Riessman, 2008). Place referred to the setting and this included the schools attended, classroom, office or staff room. I coded anything that actually occurred as an event. Characters included teachers, teaching assistant staff, headmaster and other important members in the school community of the storyteller's life and story. Time represented a period that a narrative had occurred and, finally, the plot referred to contradictions and defining moments that moved the story along. These five elements informed the narrative helping tell the story, as it developed over the course of the interview (see table 4). I analysed each interview separately, isolating and highlighting the narrative elements, keeping the narratives intact

16

(Neilson, 1984). Therefore, I looked at the extracts depicted in a narrative, identified the narrative elements (i.e., characters, place, time, event, plot) and then named the underlying understandings of the narrative instead of coding line-by-line.

Narrative Thematic Elements	Definitions	Examples from Data
Place	Where did the event take place?	Dawn: We had around 27-30 pupils in a class. The numbers impacted learning. I grew up in a socially deprived area and a lot of the children had learning difficulties. There was a lot of fighting and displays of bad behaviour. Teachers found it difficult to manage the behaviour and lessons were disrupted as the teacher went off to get the headmaster.
Event	What happened?	Dylan: When the White teachers talked their foolishness, for example, Egyptians were White, I would challenge them and this is one of the reasons as to why I got expelled.
Characters	Who was involved?	Dylan: When I was expelled from school, I left church. I did not like the Orthodox teaching. The Black preacher was teaching the same foolishness as the White teachers.
Time	Chronological placement	Dylan: I was in the top sets for English, the first year I was in 1:1, second year, 2:1, third year, 3:1, fourth year, 4:1, fifth year,5.1. I started questioning the teachers which landed me in 5:3. That was where the pupils were more disruptive than anything else.
Plot	Contradictions or defining moments	Douglas: We sat at desks in rows. You could choose where you wanted to sit. I mixed with pupils from other ethnic backgrounds but because there were not very many Black pupils, I mainly interacted with White pupils. A self-service choice of seating was better as you could avoid sitting with someone disruptive. I am not sure how this impacted my performance as it was normal at the time.

Table 4
A coding map for the narrative thematic analysis

This study also considered secondary sources and I applied a systematic review of the existing literature on the academic performance of Black pupils in England. The literature was identified using combinations of terms such as: curricula, pedagogy, disadvantaged, attainment, racism, barriers to progress etc. A pattern matching procedure predicting the outcomes based on theoretical propositions was used (Saunders, 2016). The propositions are analysed in the data analysis process. This procedure involves the development of an analytical framework which uses existing theories to test how adequate it is in explaining the findings. If a pattern is actually found as was predicted, then it is evidence to suggest that there is an explanation for the results.

Coding Process

After I completed transcribing the data, I listened to the tape recorder to double-check for accuracy. Re-reading the transcript enabled me to notice contradictions and sections that reflected the storyteller's complex sociocultural history. What is more, repeat reading also allowed me to attend to the different voices that make up individual sections that make up the story (Kim, 2015).

Construction of Narrative Accounts. After completing the analyses for each participant's story, I recreated narrative accounts of their experiences with the curriculum and pedagogical approach. The notes written during the interview and coding process informed my writing of the narrative accounts. I used the notes as a trail to other paths of the story's meaning. This helped me capture pieces of the participant's narratives that were unfolding during the interview.

Moving from Story to Story. As I worked from story to story, I repeated the same coding process, using the coding map for each narrative for consistency. I continued writing notes and spotted when familiar patterns and connections from one story connected to the next. Rather than avoid contaminating the ideas of one story to the next, I used notes to spot and acknowledge these connections. I used the notes written during the analysis process to inform the final level of analysis, where I collectively analysed the stories.

Shared Narrative Meaning. As I collectively analysed the stories, I cross-referenced the narrative accounts for shared narrative meaning. According to Clandinin (2000), shared narrative meaning is the common threads among the stories. I reread each narrative account and laid them alongside each other to identify recurring threads. What narratives presented in each of the accounts? What echoed across the storytellers' experiences? Thereafter, I drew connections between the stories. Clandinin (2000) further defines threads as echoes across the data. Figure 2 depicts the coding process as a pyramid between the various levels of analysis. The initial coding consisted of the narrative thematic analysis: this was followed by the construction of narrative accounts that interwove the analyses: finally, I identified connections and narrative meaning across the narrative accounts.

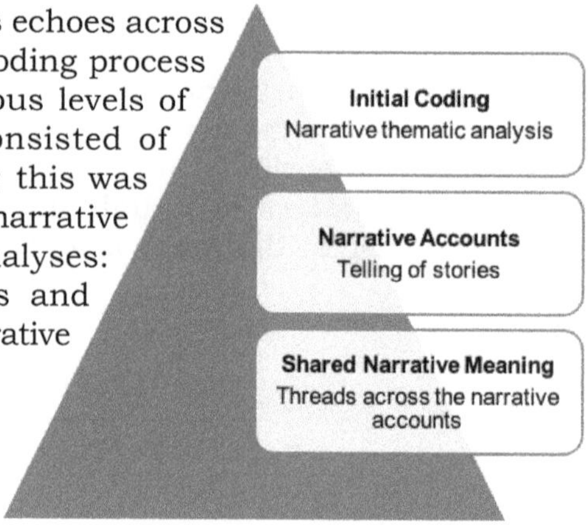

Figure 2
Three levels of analysis

Rigour and Trustworthiness

There are several ways one can build rigour and trustworthiness. According to Guba & Lincoln (1989), trustworthiness involves building credibility, transferability and dependability. Credibility is the extent to which the findings can be trusted and considered credible research. Transferability is a means by which we determine how relatable or transferable the findings are to the experiences of others who fit in the community we are interested in. Dependability is the consistency between data and results. It is also the initial coding narrative thematic and narrative accounts. Furthermore, dependability is the telling of the told, the shared narrative meaning and threads across the narrative accounts (see Figure 2). There are various strategies one can adopt for building trustworthiness, for instance triangulation, taking notes and for this study, table 5 lists the methods used to improve credibility, transferability and dependability.

	Definition	Methods
Credibility	How can the findings be trusted	• Researcher's lived experiences • Note taking • Black community advisory group • Prolonged engagement • Triangulation of data collection and analysis
Transferability	How can the results be consistent with the data	• Audit trail and documentation of analytic responses • Narrative coherence • Triangulation of data collection and analysis
Dependability	How can the findings relate to others' experiences	• Purposive sampling • Thick description of the social and cultural context of each participant's experience • Triangulation of data collection and analysis

Table 5
The building of Trustworthiness in this study

Triangulation. The triangulation of data was facilitated by the collection of multiple forms of data, including: interviews, literature review and note taking. Different data sources were collected at different points in time, through different means and analysed using different approaches. From the point of view of a social constructivist paradigm, triangulation of data collection and data analysis help the researcher understand the data in a more reliable way by paying attention to the diverse social construction of realities. This also complements the narrative interview concept of polyphony that privileges multiple interpretations and voices within the data (Kim, 2015). Triangulation is often used to increase credibility, transferability and dependability.

Researcher's Lived Experiences. As a mother of 4 children ranging between 2 and 20 years of age, 3 of whom have attended state school, my experiences helped me through the interviews. This improved the project's credibility. My involvement in the children's academic work: helping out in the classroom, accompanying the children to school trips, etc., all helped me understand a Black person's schooling experience. This equipped me with the skills to develop researcher-participant relationships, construct useful follow-up questions, think conversationally and determine the risks and vulnerability that participants might experience in the research process. As a Black woman, who emigrated from Uganda to England, I had my own experiences with oppression. Thus, I was conscious of my biases and beliefs and held myself accountable for my part in the relationship with participants, by remaining impartial and taking relational responsibility.

Black Community Advisory Group. Local parents from the community of interest acted as advisers, but were not participants in the study. After designing the interview questions, I presented them to this group and asked them to check the language of the interviews for cultural sensitivity. This group of advisors included four parents, 2 identified as African and 2 Afro-Caribbean. One critical piece of this process was learning, from these advisors, how to take language into account when interviewing and having the manoeuvrability to ask questions differently, based on the participant's cultural context.

Prolonged Engagement. According to Guba & Lincoln (1985), having prolonged engagement with the group of interest establishes a relationship of trust between the researcher and participants. I interacted with the participants for a period of up to 6 months. The majority of participants indicated interest in being a part of similar projects in the future and I have remained in contact with a small number of them. Although there could have been more prolonged engagement with each participant, narrative interview is deeply ethical and thinking narratively is also thinking relationally. In the majority of times, narrative inquirers become a part of the landscapes they study (Clandinin, 2013). Following on from this, I have used this project as a stepping stone for my PhD, where I am currently exploring the lived experiences of Black LGBTQ+ students in higher education institutes in the UK, North America and South Africa.

Audit trail and documentation of analytic responses. I conducted an audit trail and documentation analytic responses in the form of notes which improved consistency and dependability of the data (Rodgers & Cowles, 1993). My very first notes were written in my first research methods lecture, where we were asked to think about our topics. I straight away thought Black boys in the English education system. Then later, during the research design phase, while writing the dissertation proposal, I thought about my son's experience in schooling, something that informed the study design. During the interview process I took notes of my thoughts and during analysis I continued writing notes to guide my analyses. Maintaining audio files, notes, transcripts and timeline data was also a part of constructing an audit trail. The careful documentation of the transcription process and data storage contributed to the dependability of the audit trail.

Narrative Coherence. Narrative coherence is the extent to which the story makes sense in context and the overall congruency of the narratives (Clandinin, 2013). Even though coherence seems impossible at times, seeking coherence is often a part of experiencing life. As a narrative inquirer, I try to accommodate both successful and unsuccessful attempts toward narrative coherence and restrain from always glossing over any disparities in the stories in the narrative accounts (Clandinin, 2013). Many of the stories shared during the interview process were traumatic and unspoken in some of the cases: something which Riessman (2008) claims can enhance narrative coherence.

Sampling and Thick Description. I conducted purposive sampling and focused on recruiting Black people who were pupils in the English education system between 1950-2000, so as to establish transferability. Indeed, for my PhD, I am exploring the lived experiences of Black students but focused on higher education and the intersectionality aspect of sexuality and gender. Thick descriptions in the narrative accounts, transparency and detailed description of the methods all improve the trustworthiness of the study.

Quality of the Study's Significance. When the findings generate information that is useful and important, trustworthiness is enhanced. According to Clanindin (2013), personal, practical and social justifications are the guide for answering the so what? and who cares? questions in a narrative interview. Personal justifications will require the researcher to position narrative interview in their own experiences, conflicts and struggles. I acknowledge that my personal justification had roots in wanting to explore the experiences of Black pupils in the English education system and equip myself with the knowledge to facilitate a better experience and results for my children. My own experience of putting my older child through state school sparked my curiosity in the stories of people who had experienced the same system prior to the year 2000. Were the experiences similar or different? Were the pupils successful or not? What do we do next? Practical justifications address the possibilities for Black pupils in this study to offload their experiences and generate narrative meaning by telling stories that are often disregarded. Data regarding the education of Black pupils is limited and I hope that the practical justifications would contribute to filling this gap and help the participants heal through sharing their stories in a safe space: sharing with a Black woman who was a parent and, just like some of them, had similar experiences. Finally, the social justification for the study was to promote the values of inclusion and equity and to ensure that Black pupils share in the higher education standards attained by the most successful pupils in schools in England.

Rationale for Methodology

The methodology employed for this study was narrative interviews which created a space for the Black pupils' stories of how they experienced schooling. Since the purpose of this study is to explore the impact of the curriculum and pedagogy on the academic performance of Black pupils, narrative interviews enabled me to: use story to explore the storytellers' entire experiences: involve the storytellers in a personal way: bear in mind the multiple stories: highlight all aspects of life in the story in a meaningful way: expand how a story is interpreted from an individual's perspective to a collective experience and explore the telling of stories as they were defined within systems of power and domination.

Limitations of Methodology

In some cases, interviews were limited in their transferability because I focused on the individual's story rather than the wider application to others in the same community of interest. What is more, language and cultural barriers may have impacted the process of telling and interpreting the stories as well as the participants' ability to comfortably convey emotional details through conversation. Language and culture may have for the researcher impacted the ability to understand what was expressed by the participant especially since the researcher's values and experiences inevitably shape the conversation and sometimes analysis. It was of the utmost importance that I resolved any issues arising in the researcher-participant relationship in order to avoid this negatively shaping the process. The use of audio recording during the interviews limited my understanding of body language and subtle expressions in the conversation that is of itself a form of data. Misunderstandings are more likely to have occurred in conversations over the telephone rather than face to face. This potentially reduced the sense of intimacy and personable quality of the interview given the technological medium. The study was limited in its scope as the focus on Black pupils meant that I could not get the perspective of White teachers who, more than likely, taught the majority of participants and whose input, especially on the issue of pedagogy, would have been valuable. The rationale for this was that I wanted to highlight the stories of a people that are often overlooked in research and this could be a suitable topic in future work. Furthermore, it is possible that someone who taught prior to 2000 had retired or would have been uncomfortable going on record.

Ethical Considerations

As the researcher, I needed to address inherent power in the researcher-participant relationship at the beginning of the study and respect and highlight the fact that the participant was an expert in their own life. Therefore, at the start of the informed consent process, I explained to the participants the aim, objectives and procedures of the study, indicating to them that they could withdraw from the study at any point with no explanation or consequences. Another ethical consideration was confidentiality and ensuring the identity of the participants remained anonymous, because some were teachers at the time or had children in schools and participation could have had negative consequences. Furthermore, it was important to take into account how emotional some participants were bound to get opening up about issues for the first time and to this effect, I offered breaks, asked if participants were well at the end of the interview and, was available to be contacted after the interview process. In addition, the use of telephone interview required the researcher and participant to agree additional steps for maintaining confidentiality, such as finding a time and place when the participant would not be interrupted or disturbed and had privacy. Correspondence between participants and researcher was managed through email which was password protected and the telephone interviews were conducted while I was alone in a private setting. I protected recorded data on a secure laptop that only I could access and the laptop was kept in the locked cupboard of the researcher. At the end of the project, the data was kept for two years after which it was destroyed. Participants were not given any incentives for taking part in the study.

Ethical Decision-Making Guide

This study was guided by the University of West London Research Ethics Code of Practice 2018. A copy of the research ethics code of practice was sent to the interviewee at least 48 hours before the interview was conducted. This was to give the participants a chance to familiarise themselves with the principles therein. At the beginning of each interview, the participant was reminded of the ethics code of practice and asked if there were any questions. Ethics principle (3.I) states that "Research should be undertaken under the basic principle that it does not cause harm, allow harm to be inflicted, or otherwise damage the interests of any parties involved". Principle (3.4) states that "Researchers have a duty to care for participants and may be held liable where this duty is breached and harm is incurred". I protected the participants' confidentiality and minimized the risk of harm by attending to the values of justice, critique and care (Shapiro & Stefkovich, 2016). Principle (3.5) states that "Any research that takes place in the public domain, or results in outcomes disseminated in the public domain, should respect cultural sensitivities and abide by decency and obscenity laws. I maintained respect at all times and notified participants when and where the results were published and gave them the necessary link to access document(s). Requirements: (4.1) states that "Any participation in a research project should normally take place in the context of a clear and unambiguous agreement between researcher(s) and participant(s). In projects which carry some risk for participants, this should normally take the form of written consent by the participant(s), with written information provided, giving explicit details of any risks". (4.2) "Participants should in most cases be given clear and unambiguous information relating to the activities in which they will be involved. Failure to fully inform participants of any known relevant factor may make consent invalid". I obtained informed consent prior to the interview and during the interview process I started off by ensuring that the participants wanted to continue with the process. (4.6) "Anonymity of participants and confidentiality must be maintained in all cases. In exceptional cases, where anonymity cannot be guaranteed, full and explicit written permission should be obtained to use images or other forms of personal data of participants. Personal data should only be disclosed in exceptional cases and with reference to the latest general data protection regulation. Specific permission should also be sought for such data to be put into the public domain, for example in an exhibition, publication or recording". I maintained anonymity and confidentiality by allocating participants with pseudonyms and keeping data under lock and key and password protected. (4.7) "Researchers should inform individuals of their rights to decline participation in a study or to withdraw at any time, without penalty, irrespective of any agreement(s) or incentives. These rights must be respected by the researcher in all circumstances and participants may require destruction of their personal data if prior permission has not been obtained – which of itself would constitute a breach of research integrity (see Research Integrity Code of Practice) and under GDPR legislation". I made the participants aware of the right to exercise their autonomy by their voluntary participation and their right to withdraw at any point of the study.

Chapter 3: Findings

Participant Demographics

All of the 22 prospective participants who viewed and signed the consent form, scheduled and completed the interview. Hence a 100% completion rate. Twelve of the participants were women (54.55%) and ten were men (45.45%). They identified as African (n = 10, 45.45%), followed by West Indian (n = 7, 31.81%), Mixed (n = 4, 18.18%) and White (n = 1, 4.54%). (See Table 6).

	Number (n)	%
Gender		
Female	12	54.55
Male	10	45.45
Ethnicity		
African	10	45.45
West Indian	7	31.81
Mixed	4	18.18
White	1	4.54

Table 6
Participant Demographics

Curriculum

For the participants the curriculum revolved around three aspects,

1) Representation within the curriculum.

2) How participants were streamed and what sets they were allocated.

3) What expectations were set for them (see figure 3).

According to the DfE, the main aim of the national curriculum is to provide pupils with an introduction to the essential knowledge they need to be educated citizens. It introduces pupils to the best that has been thought and said and helps engender an appreciation of human creativity and achievement. However, the participants testified to being taught the best that has been thought and said by White people and a Eurocentric curriculum that had no one that looked like them represented by it.

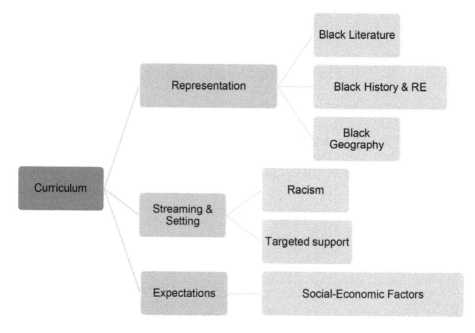

Figure 3
Curriculum

Pedagogy

For the participants, pedagogy centred around four aspects:

1) Teaching techniques experienced.

2) Classroom size.

3) Classroom set-up.

4) Teacher-Pupil relationship (see figure 4).

The participants reported varying experiences as we will see from their stories below.

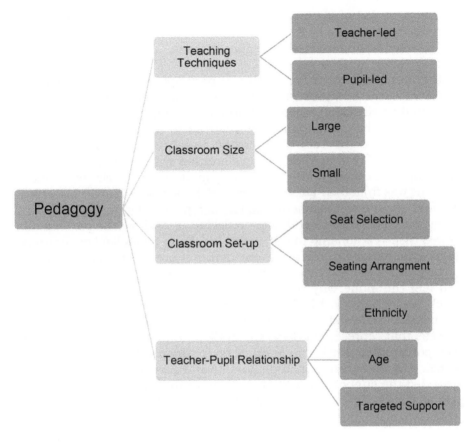

Figure 4
Pedagogy

Narrative Accounts and
Selected Sub-Themes

Over a period of six months, I talked with twenty-two participants from different regions in England. To follow, are the narrative accounts and selected subthemes, which captivated me.

The narrative accounts include the participants' narrative thematic and structural analyses. They provide a fuller picture of the data through the use of storytelling and bringing together the coded elements. Quotes from the participants are referred to as Interviews. Several subthemes emerged from the thematic and structural analyses of the participants. These included representation within the subjects they were taught: streaming and setting, mainly in the core subjects: expectations (and this was from their teachers or parents): the teaching style: classroom size and seating arrangement: the teacher-pupil relationship including teacher access. These subthemes reflected upon how the participants viewed their relationship to self, peers, teachers, family and community. Some experiences described were monumental. For example, some participants were told by a teacher that they were not good enough and still feel the same way today or the experience of having that one Black teacher that a Black student could run to for anything. Some participants reflected on how important it was to have role models of success that represented them culturally, not just White people. Some even contemplated living in another body because they were ashamed of their African heritage, including name and accent. Some participants identified the support they needed, whether that was from the teacher, peer or family. This is all in the stories that follow:

Dawn's Story

Representation. I was missing from the curriculum. I did not see characters or language that I could identify with. If English was your first language you did not need to understand the structure. However, if it is not, this makes it difficult to understand the structure and how other languages work. This especially affected my ability to learn other languages like French when I was at school.

Streaming and Settings. I was in top sets for English. I loved books but, due to family difficulties, I missed a lot of school and I was moved down to the bottom sets where people struggled to spell their names or had a mild learning disability like dyslexia. I felt like this was unfair because missing school was out of my control as a child. Within two years they moved me back up because I was doing everyone's homework for them. This negatively impacted my o-level results. I think sets are fine because different people work at different levels, as long as everyone has the opportunity to move up a level when they are ready. Sets should not be used as punishment for unsuitable behaviour. My son was moved from a top set (red) table to a lower set (orange) table and the reason was that the child who had moved to the top was disruptive, my child was upset by this. I went into the school, the teacher was dismissive and said, we do not differentiate based on tables. My son has gone on to do very well but it was that at the whim of the teacher, he was taken away from his position in a place where he felt that he had worked really hard and deserved to be. This had an effect on his confidence for a long time. Sets should be fair.

Expectations. The school had very low expectations for Black pupils. I really wanted to do office skills, short hand or typing but I was told that this wouldn't be suitable for me, instead I was allocated home economics which I didn't enjoy and I still don't enjoy to this day. I felt very much that they were trying to pigeon-hole me and push me towards a career in caring or cleaning and doing domestic work. One of the teachers said that I could be a domestic if I was looking for a career option. I thought this was insulting, not to say being a domestic is not a good job but the fact that she thought that there were no other career options for me. I think I did okay at school but she had such a low opinion of me that I could not reach a particular level above just cleaning floors and bathrooms.

Teaching Techniques. Mine was predominantly a teacher led style. The teacher was at the board, giving you, information and you copied this and occasionally did some group work. Teachers were allowed to punish or cane so I was very frightened of them. I would sit quietly, watch the board and listen to the teacher. I am a visual learner. I like to see things. I think other ways of learning are better other than chalk and blackboard. For instance, a more varied approach where we could come up with ideas ourselves in groups. It would have been better if we had a chance to think before the teacher gave us the information and role play to get the message across. Science should have been much more hands-on rather than sitting down and listening to a teacher. Science should be more feeling rather than listening. I think I did okay at school but I had a very difficult childhood. I missed a lot of school. Teachers were always angry with me and they shouted at me a lot. There was a lot of bullying going on and I didn't have the voice to say "you are bullying me" so that made me more reluctant to go to school. I would hope that teachers are more understanding these days.

Classroom Size. We had around 27-30 pupils in a class. The numbers impacted learning. I grew up in a socially deprived area and a lot of the children had learning difficulties. There was a lot of fighting and displays of bad behaviour. Teachers found it difficult to manage the behaviour and lessons were disrupted as the teacher went off to get the headmaster. The boys would be fighting with chairs thrown across the room. It is therefore important for teachers in that type of a situation to think about the type of children they have in a class and how they are going to manage them. You can't have a whole class highjacked for half an hour waiting for the headmaster to intervene. Time in lessons is limited.

Classroom Set-up. In my son's class, it was a round table setting but all students knew that pupils sitting at the top table were better. While I was at school, we had desks in rows and we just faced the board. Some people sat at the back while others sat at the front. The ones at the back were sometimes missed. I was seated in the middle: it was a catholic school: there was no mixing of ethnic origin. All Asians stuck together and White, Irish, West Indian and Africans alike. There were cliques and we could not mix.

Teacher-Pupil Relationship. I don't remember accessing a teacher, because I found them intimidating and frightening. A teacher bullied me to a point that other students stood up to defend me. If I didn't put my hand up, he would scream in my face and he would do the same if I got the answer wrong. As soon as lessons finished, I would just disappear and go home. That particular teacher behaved that way towards me because he didn't have control of the class or the respect of the students. I think he wanted to make an example of me: There were incidents where police were involved. Teachers had abused a Black child who refused to take her clothes off to do PE: this was in the papers. I don't recall having a relationship with any teacher: I would come in and leave quietly. I tried not to draw attention to myself. It massively impacted me. I left school with no qualifications. I didn't have a good relationship with any teachers. They weren't interested in me as an individual and I didn't spend any time at school but I love learning and I knew that I had the capacity. When I left school, I went to college and did my nursing training and a nursing degree. I carried on doing things. I think everyone has the ability and teachers just have to encourage and support the pupils, to achieve to their potential. They need to find out what and where problems are and help. Pedagogy most impacted my academic performance.

David's Story

Representation. What I found very beneficial when I came back to the UK was the availability of the equipment to experiment while doing physics. This was something I didn't have access to before. It was new and what I found was that the students here didn't take advantage of these resources.

Streaming and Settings. I moved back to England at college age and cannot remember experiencing being placed in sets.

Expectations. The expectations set for me were very much set by my parents, certainly not the school. My parents set high expectations for me. It was always something I knew: that I had to achieve high standards in those exams. A was the highest grade you could get and I was clear from the start that this is what I was expected to get in all my A-level subjects. Having those expectations drove me to high achievement. If I hadn't had those expectations upon me, I don't think that I would have necessarily been self-motivated at that time, as a teenage boy, to deliver to that standard, but knowing that that was what was expected of me from a family angle, I knew that I had to deliver and not disappoint my family.

Teaching Techniques. It was a directive style of teaching. The teacher imparted information and you were expected to absorb it and process the information. Except economics where I remember there being a dialogue in class. The teacher gave us more space to bring our own thoughts and ideas to the discussion. Not necessarily that he would always agree with them and in some situations, he explained why he thought our views were flawed. But he would always seek our input as part of the teaching experience. I guess the directive teaching style is what I was used to. It didn't feel unnatural and I did feel comfortable with it. This worked well with maths. However, I did find that with physics, I couldn't rely purely on what I had covered in the lessons. I was very comfortable with things being taught in a lesson and taking that away and absorbing it. What I found with A-level physics was that I had to go and do more of the reading on my own to supplement what was being taught and that was something that I realised over time. The exams were harder than I was used to and in the second year of my A-levels, I do recall having to read more on my own to make sure that I had covered everything in sufficient detail and I managed to maintain the standard I had expected. In the end I was able to deliver the objectives I had set myself so I don't think it impacted my performance. When I look back, a couple of things I noticed, 1-When I came into the course, I had to present my assessment and course materials from my former school in Africa to my current school in England. They didn't accept it as sufficient so I had to sit another set of exams before I did my A-levels for them to be able to confirm to their satisfaction that I was able to do the course. 2-There was not an attempt to understand my aspirations and what I wanted to do in terms of university courses. Whilst I did have discussions with careers staff in terms of university applications and particularly the likes of Oxford and Cambridge, in the end I did not apply and it is something I regret. I think there could have been a bit more encouragement for me to be more ambitious in my choice of university going forward.

Classroom Size. There were anywhere upwards of 15 in a class and maybe a few more in economics. With the maths and physics lessons, it was not so much the numbers but that you had quite a range of abilities within that. You had people trying to work hard to get an E-grade and on the other end people like myself who were trying to get an A-grade. When you have people of that breadth of ability in a class it is a challenge for the teacher to teach the material at the right level. This did not affect my performance because I learnt to go away and fill in the gaps to the level of detail that I wanted to cover but it did require me to do that to deliver.

Classroom Set-up. We sat in rows. It was a traditional set up for both maths and physics. In economics, it was u-shaped and the teacher would sort of move around and, as I said, that was much of a discussive thing. I didn't think about it much at the time. I guess it was that with the hard sciences, it was the teacher's job to impart the knowledge and for us to receive it. Whereas with the social science of economics again not to say Black or White, an interactive teaching style is probably more beneficial. When it came to pupils from different backgrounds there was not much mixing. I socialised with people on the grounds of sport or people from the Caribbean.

Teacher-Pupil Relationship. I can't remember ever having to access the teacher so am not sure how accessible they would have been or indeed whether they could have made more of an effort to provide on a one-to-one basis. I didn't seek the teachers because I didn't need to. I was getting the grades I needed so there was no need and it was something I had never been used to. The teacher called you: you didn't go to them. I had people I mixed with in a social, sport and academic context. I'm not sure groups impacted my performance. I remember my economics teacher mainly because of his participative style. We had a good relationship. I think he had time for me and very good input. I remember the very first test I did in economics where I got 25 out of 25 and he came up to me and told me that no one had ever got this mark. He said I clearly had potential in the subject and that he needed to make sure I achieved to my potential. He did have time for me and not only in a classroom setting. The maths teacher, I remember, he spent the majority of time with people who needed the help and guidance. I thought I got what I needed from him and not anything more. All were good but the physics teacher who I would rank third as he spent almost all his time with the students who needed his help. The relationship with my economics teacher impacted my love for the subject and also the fact that I did go on to do a degree in economics. My interest in the subject was very much fostered by his interest in my personal life, learning and understanding of the course. I was most impacted by pedagogy.

Daniel's Story

Representation. In history we learnt about, Europe, World War I, World War II, America, early 20th century, great depression, Ku Klux Klan. I thought the content was decent. The older materials like the Tudors, I found very boring. The modern stuff was good because it covered recent stuff that was relatable to our day to day lives. I didn't like geography, music, or art. I didn't find history interesting to start with so I dropped it, but I picked it up again and actually it was my best GCSE. I found the teacher more interesting than all the ones before. Up to year 9, in history, we had to learn and write long answers but for my GCSE, the answers weren't actually that long, I preferred short answers, 12 marks instead of 30-mark questions, focused learning.

Streaming and Settings. I was in top sets in maths and this was good because the class could move faster. You spent less time on the syllabus because you could fit it all in whereas some people, especially in the lower sets, needed more time. Being in the top set makes you competitive: I liked getting top marks in the class or at least I tried to get the same grades as my peers. In a bigger class, it was easier to get top marks than it is with a smaller group. I was in the top or middle set in English and it was still competitive: I worked hard to get the top marks. Sets have been beneficial to me. Without sets, I wouldn't have tried hard.

Expectations. My school set high expectations: they predicted A*s for all my GCSEs and they do that for the majority of people. It was stressful because they predict grades instead of focusing on just trying to pass. Because of this pressure I took down a lot of notes in subjects such as chemistry and physics and I did well. However, in biology, I did not do as much revision and notes and I did not do as well. I didn't find biology that enjoyable so am not sure how much that really helps.

Teaching Techniques. We got given a lot of information and you had to learn it. Sometimes it was interactive like board games, to test your knowledge. That I found interesting. There was also group work and projects. I am not really a fan of projects. In my religious studies GCSE, my mark reduced to A from an A* because the project work counted for 20%. Project work requires a lot of detail. I found it quite difficult and hard to go between different sources. In maths and physics, there was not much room for individuality. These were the equations you needed to know. Sometimes we did projects in physics and this was participative. Subjects that require writing an essay present one with more room to have an individual point of view and you do not have to stick to what the teacher tells you. In some of the really complex stuff you have to stick to what the teacher tells you. I was best at doing what I was told when there was a manageable amount of content. However, where subjectivity was involved and there is no wrong or right answer then it is impossible to stick with what you are told. Notes were boring. Some teachers did not give you time to write them all down. I liked practicing questions, instead of just talking about stuff and then practicing. I think individual teachers, impacted my performance. Some subjects were more interesting than others. Teachers can make a subject less or more boring just with the way they speak about it. When a teacher is interesting, you pay more attention and remember a lot more. In French we had varied teaching styles, for example: the use of electronic websites, writing and reporting and I still managed to get an A.

Classroom Size. Our classroom had 30 pupils. The smaller classes are nicer because you get more access to the teacher. If you have a specific question, you can ask with ease. However, the more people there are in a room, the more of a discussion you can have and it is nice to compare your marks to someone else's.

Classroom Set-up. There was a teacher's desk and sometimes an interactive blackboard. I usually sat in rows at a desk. In class, I sometimes interacted with whoever I was sitting next to. In some classes there was a sitting plan. Outside of class I would not say I interacted with many people from a similar background as there were not many in my school. At one point there were 4 Black pupils and that decreased to 2 as they went to a different college. So, I mainly interacted with Asian children. I liked sitting at the back but with poor vision, I had to sit in the middle so I could see the board clearly. It was enormous pressure sitting in the front so preferred the back. Sitting in the front was sometimes more enjoyable. The teacher would look over your head and you would pretend you were writing. Some teachers were strict and they chose where you sat. I wouldn't say where I sat had a massive impact but I guess outside of lessons it had a personal and social impact which affected you and ended up affecting your performance as well. Sometimes you felt like you could not relate to people around you but I wonder if they were all Black, whether I would struggle to relate. I am not sure.

Teacher-Pupil Relationship. We had email addresses for all our teachers. Different teachers replied at different times to emails. For Religious studies we had 3 different teachers who reacted. I wanted to visit teachers in their office but it was not reliable as you don't know when they were going to be in. For most of my education, I was afraid of teachers because I thought they were going to punish me, if I did not pay attention or finish my work. But as I got older, they got more relaxed and I guess I had a more casual relationship with them. I would not say we were friends: I was still respectful. We had small talk, where teachers knew stuff about me. Younger teachers were more interesting because some had similar schooling experiences. White teachers were more accessible to White students because of less cultural differences. I think

Asian teachers were quite relatable in some situations. Some teachers were very strict and it did not help. I would rush my work instead of just admitting to my teacher and asking to hand the work in the next day when I had enough time to get it done properly. The less strict a teacher is, the more approachable they are. Teachers should be more lenient, then pupils are more likely to work harder. Also, teachers should try and focus on the big and not small stuff.

Douglas' Story

Representation. Back then I wasn't aware. I didn't enjoy school and I just wanted to get out. The subjects didn't relate to me. More could have been done to gear things towards my interests and abilities. More could have been done to encourage Black students to work harder.

Streaming and Settings. I hated school anyway. I just did what I had to do and get out of there. This was the 80s. There was racism, you had to fight that and try and get an education at the same time. I was put in a low maths group but I was getting 99% and for some reason I wasn't able to move up a level. The result of this is that I could only get a certain grade in my exam. Once you were put in a low grade, that was it. There was no need to work harder and you were not encouraged too either. Streaming is wrong. I was assessed at 13 for a pre-determined target grade for when I was 16. There was no scope for improvement at any given time in that three years at school.

Expectations. There were no expectations set for Black or White pupils that weren't high achievers. Once a pupil was identified as medium or low achiever, there was no encouragement to achieve higher. This had a negative impact on the academic performance of any pupil that wanted to know more.

Teaching Techniques. We were taught to pass exams. If you asked a question, you were told you did not need to know. It was something I didn't agree with at the time. There was no encouragement for you to broaden your knowledge more than was in the curriculum.

Classroom Size. 30-32 pupils were normal in my class. I would have preferred smaller classes because you get more one to one time with the teacher. You would also get more attention and time to ask questions.

Classroom Set-up. We sat at desks in rows. You could choose where you wanted to sit. I mixed with pupils from other ethnic backgrounds but because there were not very many Black pupils, I mainly interacted with White pupils. A self-service choice of seating was better as you could avoid sitting with someone disruptive. I am not sure how this impacted my performance as it was normal at the time.

Teacher-Pupil Relationship. I did not access any of my teachers because I hated school. I didn't feel that I was getting enough out of it. I found the lessons quite boring and we weren't taught anything relevant at the time or useful to me as a teenager. I just wanted to get out and leave. Also, we were not encouraged to approach teachers. There was no relationship or understanding of who I was by anyone in school. The teacher relationship most impacted me.

Dorothy's Story

Representation. I was young. I did what I was told by my teachers and followed my parents' wishes: The order was focus on the core subjects, select some from the optional ones and proceed to college. The syllabus was set and you just followed. The curriculum is different now, with subjects such as graphic design and web design, that I would have liked to do. I also wish I had the opportunity to specialise in something like public health. It would have saved a lot of time.

Streaming and Settings. I was in sets for the core subjects. I was in the middle set for English, bottom for maths: I struggled. I was happy with this arrangement because we all learn differently. However, sets can be limiting especially for slow learners.

Expectations. The school had low expectation of me because I had just come from another country and I had an accent. They thought I was not up-to-standard compared to someone that had grown up in the system. I was depressed. It knocks you and has a huge impact on your life. My academics suffered and I missed out. Your school days are supposed to be the happiest. But when that is not right, the foundation is weak and the future is bleak. I wish I had one-to-one support from my teachers, maybe during out of hours. I can't blame the teachers because this is probably how they were taught. Maybe they did not know how to deal with students.

Teaching Techniques. It was a teacher-led style. The teacher delivered and you put your hand up if you had a question. With English as an additional language, I did not understand some words and the teacher could have explained a bit more. It would have been helpful if the teacher explained what we were going to do and why. It is a lot to ask but I think slow learners would have benefited from this. In addition, having English as second language meant that you had to understand English first, in order to understand other subjects. So, there was a need for extra support. If these issues are not resolved at the outset then, the student's performance suffers going forward.

Classroom Size. There were between 25-30 pupils in a class and of this maybe 5 were Black. The different groups stuck together. It was difficult having come from a different country. The Black kids that were born in England interacted together and I felt isolated. I had an accent and I was bullied. Looking back, I wish I didn't have an accent and I was more confident. The problem was that I didn't look or sound the same. I didn't fit in: something that negatively affected my performance and life to this day.

Classroom Set-up. We sat at tables in a row. The teachers stood at the front. I intentionally sat myself at the back because I felt that was where I belonged: I was shy: I did not fit in: I wasn't worthy: and I could hide, especially in maths. I enjoyed religious education and sat in the middle so I could see and hear what the teacher was saying. If I was a teacher, I would look out for those pupils acting differently. I would pay attention and try and find out why. When it comes to supporting Black pupils, for some teachers, race influences their decisions. They struggle especially if they come from a different background. They can be apprehensive and afraid of you and sometimes they do not know what to say. Back then race was an issue. Thinking about it all, seating arrangement had a significant negative impact on my academic performance.

Teacher-Pupil Relationship. I did not think out of hours were available. You just got on with your work. I was young, I was not confident and I could not speak to teachers. This impacted my performance especially in maths. When I had just come to the country, my mother put me in a private school and there I had access to one-to-one support. I felt I could express myself. Teachers were helpful and they stayed behind after school. Unfortunately, we didn't have the funds to continue and the change to state school negatively impacted my life. I was most impacted by pedagogy.

Diane's Story

Representation. I did the core subjects. History and geography were not balanced and it is not balanced today. For example, we studied North America and Europe and very little African History. Not detailed enough. It is not fair and does not make sense. I would have liked to learn more about the challenges that African countries faced during the 18th century and imperialism. The curriculum should be updated. If you are really into the subject and passionate about it, for example history, you want your country represented. It is also equally as important if you did not grow up there. For example, children that migrate to Britain when they are young. They want to learn about what their country of origin is like. This is mainly because the national curriculum should deliver for all.

Streaming and Settings. Sets were different from what they are today but the concept was similar. Higher sets did the pure sciences, intermediate, were in between and lower sets had integrated science which was easier. I was in top sets. I am in between when it comes to sets because teachers cannot deliver equally to a class of 30. With the little time that teachers have, they can only offer personalised learning to small groups. With a bigger class, the ones that pick up quickly will succeed and vice versa. With the lower sets sometimes, the class was smaller in size which meant that the teacher could help. However, the lower sets can be limiting as the students are told that they cannot do some subjects: for example, pure sciences and this is done at a very early age, year 9 which is irreversible damage. They should give the children a chance to grow up before such decisions are made. The kids in the lower sets fall into two types, 1) I have been told that I can't do better so what is the point in trying and 2) the ones that keep working hard but do not get moved up and they end up discouraged. Schools should do better to encourage kids in the lower sets to aspire to move up. If I were to design sets, I would keep the top sets the same and change the approach for the bottom sets. I would offer more personalised teaching and involve parents a lot more. There were more Black pupils in the bottom sets because the parent involvement is limited. Most Black parents would not have gone to school in England and so they did not have a clue and were unable to help their children. In addition, most Black people work menial jobs where they cannot control their hours and so cannot be at the school meeting otherwise, they will lose their job. It is a Catch 22. The parents do not have time to sit down with their children to find out what is going on at school. They usually find out when it is too late. Even when they manage to go to parents' evening, it is 10 minutes and once a term. Teachers could do more. They could contact parents earlier and go through the areas that the child is struggling with. Most parents that I have as a private tutor are those whose children at GCSE level cannot even do times tables which are taught in year 4 or 5.

Because the foundation was not laid properly, this is dumped on me to sort out. So, in the Black community, besides language barriers, parents do not have the knowledge capital to help their kids progress.

Expectations. When I did my A-levels, most Black students came from East London and from a less privileged background. The expectations were low. I was unlucky because, coming from Africa, teachers thought very little of me and I was lumped in with everybody else. I had to work my way out. Children look up to teachers and if they say that a pupils cannot do something, they take it to heart and will not even try. It affects your academic performance and future. Expectations should be high for everyone, in Africa, everyone is pushed to achieve higher and when you get here and the expectations are low, you relax and this took me from an A* to A student.

Teaching Techniques. Because I knew my subjects very well, I did not wait to be asked. I would volunteer my answers. So, the more outspoken you were, the more they would involve you but if you were shy, you were left behind. This very much also depended on the type of the teacher facilitating the class. If they did not care for all children, some were excluded and they were left feeling like they did not matter. That is where the classroom size is important. Class sizes should be reduced for effectiveness. Because there is no way that one facilitator can ensure that 30 pupils are happy learning. This is where teaching assistants could come in. For the style, I would have preferred a mixture of teacher and pupil-led teaching because people learn differently.

Classroom Size. The classroom size was small and this was good for support. The teacher knew everybody in terms of strengths and weaknesses. This offered positive competition: you were more engaged and wanted to get a higher mark. The discussions flowed easier. Teachers were accessible, but in the lower grades, it would have been impossible to get in touch with a teacher. For example, one teacher for year 6,7 and 8 with thirty pupils in each class: it would make it impossible. A teaching assistant could have helped both in and out of classroom.

Classroom Set-up. It was tables in rows. I sat anywhere. Usually at the back, I did not concentrate as much. A lot of Black students were seated at the back. They were distracted and did not focus. I do not know why but Black students tend to cluster and sit together. They stuck with their own because they identified with each other. The mentality in school is that Black children are so naughty so they sometime play up to this expectation. As a teacher, you should mix all the kids up, move them to the front and give them attention. Children miss out from learning from each other when they are segregated. We all have different strength and weakness and how can we share if we are separated? Schools should have a buddy system.

Teacher-Pupil Relationship. The teacher relationship was strictly professional. I would ask for help, or books. There was not much of a conversation. When they tried, the teacher would talk about Africa but not in a comfortable way. I did not feel like I belonged. The teachers did not care to know more about me. I just felt like I was there to learn and get out. This meant that teachers could not help if there was an issue because they did not know the students. Most of the naughty kids have some underlying issue: maybe they are being bullied but because this relationship does not exist teachers cannot help. Also, the teachers would not be able to communicate effectively with a parent if they did not know much about the child. With the parent's consent I try to find out about my student's life outside the classroom because this impacts their learning. This way, I can help then fully. My teachers could have attended community events and got cultural awareness training as part of their degree. I was most impacted by pedagogy.

Dylan's Story

Representation. African and Caribbean people were totally absent from the curriculum both at primary or secondary levels. There was no representation. The national curriculum states that every child should be taught the folk ways and morals that represent them ethnically and culturally. This affected me and how I felt as a Black or African person. I was learning African history well until I was seventeen. My take on Africa was different from all those other boys in school. When the White teachers talked their foolishness, for example, Egyptians were White, I would challenge them and this is one of the reasons as to why I got expelled. I didn't have the maturity to deal with them so I got confrontational. When I was expelled from school, I left the church. I did not like the Orthodox teaching. The Black preacher was teaching the same foolishness as the White teachers. African children should see representation. For example, when teaching about the British Empire, you should talk about the people that were subjects to the British Empire and what they were before Imperialism. There needs to be a balance. I was expelled at 15 and I started to attend Black History lessons. There weren't many students that attended these lessons. For me, it was during these lessons that I was taught about my African and Caribbean history, I was Introduced to famous writers like J. A. Rogers, something that has stayed with me.

Streaming and Settings. Even though I was in top sets for everything, I hated maths. I struggled with it and that was because of the way it was taught. I know this because of someone I met when I was at college who was a maths teacher. I said, I hate maths and she said, you don't hate maths. It is the way it was taught. She got a carton and explained mathematics to me in half an hour. It is about who teaches it and how they impart that information. I was in the top sets for English, the first year I was in 1:1, second year, 2:1, third year, 3:1, fourth year, 4:1, fifth year, 5:1. I started questioning the teachers which landed me in 5:3, that was where the pupils were more disruptive than anything else. I was in high sets until I started questioning teachers which saw me demoted from 1st set to 3rd set. The teachers weren't equipped to deal with my questions. Have a way to separate children that want to learn from those that don't. Sets are problematic if they are based on class, gender or race. In addition, some children are a year younger than their peers depending on the month they were born and sometimes children are lumped together regardless of what different subjects or topics they are good at.

Expectations. Expectations set for Black pupils were low and it qualitatively has not changed. When I read the autobiography of Malcom-X, he said he told his teachers he wanted to be lawyer and they said to him no. Become a carpenter. Jesus was a carpenter. In school I was told that I was as thick as two planks yet I was in top sets. I was out-scoring everyone in my class, especially in English. I smashed them all in literature. I have a great appetite for reading yet they are telling me I can't think. Dissonance causes dissonance. On one hand you are doing it. On the other, they are saying you are not. All because of the colour of your skin. Even now when you go to schools, or universities, they have low expectations for Black students and the so called Black Asian and Minority Ethnic students or students who are of a particular class. This also contributed to my exclusion from school because what they thought of me was not how I thought of myself. As a teacher I don't tell Black students that they have to work twice as hard but that they just have to go for whatever it is they want. In the programme where I work with young people, I tell them that when you know you have the ability and yet you still don't get the rewards. Then you have to look at the system.

Teaching Techniques. The teaching styles that I enjoyed are the ones I have used as a teacher. It is effective to involve the students in what they are learning in one way or another. As a student I enjoyed the engaging style of Mr. Cleo and Mr. Samuel, the only Black teacher in the school. Learning is about who teaches you and how they teach you. I enjoy involving students into what they are learning. They do little projects that we include in lessons. They will bring in examples from say, YouTube or a newspaper. I prepare my students for whatever the lesson is about. For me, it is about the engagement.

Classroom Size. Today, I ban my students from seating at the back. I do not want them absentminded or on their phones while I teach.

Classroom Set-up. Teachers control the school space and they will determine your outcome, so I tell Black parents to prepare their children so they know when to challenge teachers and when not to. Brief your children and debrief them as you are sending them into an enemy environment. My head teacher at primary school was racist. She convinced my father to send us to a state school instead of a grammar school citing that we would not fit in. My parents did not know that teachers were against Black students. Teacher training courses should have cultural awareness training. It has been pointed out that failure of Black pupils is due to White middle-class teachers who are women. I did my own research and found out that there is a big leap between primary and secondary school because pupils go from being a big fish to a small fish in the sea. Schools do not have much in place for these transitions. Kids need to experience whatever it is: let them experience secondary school while still at primary school and universities such as Cambridge and Oxford while they are still at secondary. These environments need to be demystified. The teacher-pupil relationship should be a give and take one. As a teacher, I am a learner too. I am not an expert in everything. I should take into consideration and incorporate students' ideas if they add value to the topic in question. There has to be a dialogue and not a monologue. This impacted us because our parents did not understand the system, especially if they came from commonwealth countries. Pedagogy is the most impactful.

Teacher-Pupil Relationship. We discussed this earlier.

Doris' Story

Representation. I don't recall learning much in primary. This was over 18 years ago. I remember learning about the Tudors in year 3 or 4. I remember Henry VIII. Not sure if this was taught but I would have liked to learn about Black history but again I am disturbed by Black history told from a White perspective because we did not have any teachers of colour. In Secondary school, I remember being taught Black history but again this was very much from an American perspective. We learnt about the civil rights movement. I don't think that it is the role of the curriculum to teach about authentic Black history because it requires them to unlearn their own bias and I do not think that it is going to happen in this society that we live in. I think Black history should come from our communities. In a real world we should be able to learn about all histories, Black, Asia, but we can't expect this from teachers. Bearing in mind that I used to be a teacher myself, I think it is impossible to teach about slavery, kings and queens of all these nations considering the schools have predominantly White pupils. I don't think my performance suffered entirely based on the lack of knowledge of my history but maybe the prejudice there was about young Black pupils in schools. There is a lot of misunderstanding of the Black child. I remember when I was in year 3 being put in detention for behavioural problems and this continued into my secondary school where I was sent to a behavioural centre in Birmingham because I was accused of being naughty and leading the class astray. It is less about knowing your history but the complexity of being a Black person because we are different. Our upbringing and a lack of understanding from the White teachers. As a Black person, we are vocal. In Jamaica, we communicate in a very different way from White people. So, if a White teacher is not culturally aware, they may receive this as threatening.

Streaming and Settings. I don't think sets work because we put the same type of child in the same group and they miss out on the peer help. Do I agree with it? No. Do I see why they use them, yes. I do not know what the equilibrium would be. If I was put in sets, I would have been in the middle, with my brother in the lower sets. He was not very academic and he struggled at school. I remember him not being able to tell the time. My mum tried everything to help him. I remember seeing more Black students in the bottom sets than White. One of the reasons is that the parents were not present. The impact of being in lower sets is that there is no push to do better. The child is labelled and they do not get to see that they might move up. The bottom sets have children with other issues. Some have special education needs that sometimes are not diagnosed. There maybe behavioural problems so your child is picking up on all these things. They could get frustrated, start lashing out which further leads to behavioural problems. There should not be bottom sets. We should have kids mixed, collaborating and working together. We should have tables with children of different abilities. When you see children at a table helping their friends, there is nothing more powerful. If anything, that child is gaining another skill. It shows that they are a leader, team player, or a good communicator. If we focus on academics then we are locking out potential and it breeds a lot of contempt.

Expectations. I do not remember what expectations were set for me.

Teaching Techniques. The teaching style was participative because we were young. We got quite involved. The style that I like is modelling. I get to see how things are done and then try them myself. With modelling I get shown how something is done, that way I know how to do it. It is helpful to see how a formula is used and then you can adapt it to you.

Classroom Size. There were about 28 pupils. I went to a very White school: there were 2 Black students and 3 from ethnic minority backgrounds. There were no problems. I had previously been attending a Black majority school and that was an experience I will talk about later.

Classroom Set-up. The classroom seats were pre-allocated. We never sat where we wanted. It was good to separate friends so the kids could learn. The seating plans were designed based on names but I think that the teacher should know the students so they can sit next to someone that is going to help them grow, not necessarily who they know. I mixed with everyone. In my first school I stuck with Black students because there was more of us. We played with the older year 6 girls and I thought that was amazing. In my second school, I stuck with this Black girl because it was all I knew and then she left and I had to mix with everyone.

Teacher-Pupil Relationship. The teachers were quite friendly. I was vocal in class. I was also the one who would make the jokes. This helped me. I did well at school. I was never muted and never realised that my voice was irritating until I got older. The teachers made me feel like that. I think all students should have equal access. My brother had a different experience to me. He really struggled. There were phone calls home. He did not have behavioural issues as such but he struggled. There were a lot of things put in place for him. He was not vocal. My mum was vocal for him. I was kind of naughty. I was always talking when I should not have been talking. School is a very structured place. Okay I will tell you what happened in my first school. Why I was moved. I was in an assembly. I was giggling with my friend and the head teacher said, "stop talking", first time, second time and third time he moved me to the front and I was still giggling and looking back at my friend. So, he stood me up, shook me and said, "will you shut up" and told me to sit down. I sat down. I went home and did not say anything and my cousin said, did you tell your mum what happened. I said no. She said you did not tell her that he shook you. I said no. My mum overheard and said, he did what? While I was sitting outside the head's office a teacher came up to me and asked what I was doing and I said my mum is in there talking to the headmaster. She said oh is this about what happened in the assembly? I said yes. So, it was evidenced that it happened but somehow, he got off and continued to be a head teacher and I moved schools. This was in year 3. But this followed me in my record and am not sure how it impacted me. On looking back, I was talking because that was who I am. My mum said that from a very young age, I would just go up to people and chat. Even now I get home and I will be talking to people and my partner will say, "can you stop talking to strangers." As an adult I can understand how frustrating it must have been for the headmaster but I was incredibly young. As a teacher, if I had that little me, I would have taken it as my obligation to understand all the personalities in the room and mould my style accordingly. In primary school the children are young and sometimes will not be able to read the signals which can differ in secondary school. This whole situation did not impact me but my brother who loved my old school. He hated the new school and resented me for a while. He missed his Black friends. I think the solution is at teacher training. For example, Teach First are looking for people who went to a good university, got a good degree and so on, to go into their programme. This is because they are about education, but personally I do not think recruitment is done for the right reasons. It is well and good to say we train people to teach but if the desire is not there, it would be very naive for us to think that every teacher is there because they love the profession. I think that is where the problem is. Teachers have to be passionate about wanting to work with young people and wanting to make them better regardless of their background. If you do not have this from the beginning of the teacher training, then it is going to be impossible after you qualify. Teach First is a very good programme if you want to become a leader. They give you a good salary but that is an incentive that is completely removed from the child. Children have to be at the centre of recruitment and why we get into teaching and not the other way around. I remember my personal statement, when I wanted to become a teacher, made the panel cry because there was so much love and passion in there. In every job I have done, the young person continues to be at the centre. Sorry, if a teacher does not have that, no unconscious bias training is going to correct this. I am very suspicious. I have seen teachers who love their subject but do not love the children. I think we need to find a happy medium. Teachers have got to make a conscious decision to get interested in the kids. The curriculum does not work for most students regardless of race because it is very much designed for the top maybe 20%. The curriculum is not fit for purpose and does not prepare people with the skills for work. Therefore, the relationship with your teacher is more crucial because they determine how you are going to digest the knowledge. They can make the difference in a child's life. I was that type of teacher. I would get kids that did not like the previous lesson because the teacher was not interested in them. It would normally be the older teachers because they do not like change. My way was, you can do it and a lot of them did well. I remember teachers for good and bad reasons and there is no in between. I remember the teacher who helped me with English at my GCSE and I went on to do English. I remember my maths teacher who moved me from the middle set into the top because I got 70% and I was able to do the higher paper. I remember that teacher because he saw what I was capable of. He believed in me. A good teacher is the most important thing.

Devine's Story

Representation. Nothing in education taught me about my culture per se. The focus was on British values but nothing from my African cultural background apart from Christianity. I would have liked to see some diversity. For example, in English, if we are reading stories, they should have represented all the different cultures, including African and Caribbean names. Being left out of the curriculum knocked my confidence. It made me less proud. I felt like my culture was not as educational for the British people. Maybe Africans and Afro-Caribbean people are not as educated in comparison to British people in the education system. In history I remember learning about Henry VIII and the royal family. I remember learning about slavery in secondary but not primary school. We watched a film about slavery and it portrayed how Black people were mis-treated and sold. It opened my eyes to the torture. I think it was good that this was taught. However, they did not teach us about the positive Black history like Black revolutions in Haiti and elsewhere. In primary school, in geography, we looked at Western cities and towns and Africa was portrayed as a village. It was embarrassing. I remember being embarrassed because of my last name whereas now I am very proud of it. I was embarrassed by the sound and how long my name is. The only time we were taught something positive was during Black history month. Even then Black history month was used to celebrate all the other cultures, for example Asian history. This took the focus away from Black people. As a teacher now, I try to identify with my Black pupils. I make lessons relatable with things they experience in their personal lives for example, I have used a book called Handa's Surprise. It is about an African girl, the names in the story are African and so are the characters. Some of the kids in my class were born and brought up in Africa and so they can relate to the hair styles, the girl carrying a basket of fruit on her head, or the mum playing with them. It is stuff like that, that gets kids interested in books. This book was provided by my school but I took it upon myself to ask the school for other Black authored books and Black related material. I make use of the internet as well and I access books online. I follow the national curriculum but if for example: I have to cover poetry with the year 1s, I look up poetry books on African animals. As long as I am sticking with the topic, I can include African examples. This is acceptable in my school because it is made up of 90% African and Afro-Caribbean students therefore it is important that their culture is included in the curriculum. The school is very clear on the fact that we should teach British values but are very welcoming of my ideas. We taught the kids about Meghan Markle being the first Black person to marry in the royal family. This was incorporated into the lesson on the royal family.

Streaming and Settings. I was in the middle sets. I remember my maths teacher telling me I was not going to pass and I was so demotivated.

How can you tell me I am not going to pass as a teacher? I felt so low about myself in maths and it has affected me to this day. I do not feel like I am good at maths. Even when I am teaching the class, I do not feel as confident. Just because that one teacher said it to me. I did feel discriminated against because other people in my class that were White were being given the support they needed and not me. The bottom sets were a mixture of White and Black students. As a teacher, I have mixed feeling about streaming because I have done a few experiments and noticed that pupils learnt a lot from each other in mixed ability groups and I found that the stronger pupils found it much easier to explain to the lower ability pupils, sometimes even better than me explaining it to them. I also realised that mixed groups were more successful because the kids were allowed to support one another. The kids felt like they had more responsibility and they solidified their knowledge by teaching somebody else. Also, the low ability child felt comfortable because it was their friend teaching them. Mixed abilities also helped the kids develop teamwork and social skills. On the other hand, sets make your work as a teacher easier because you can focus on fewer pupils but it is how it knocks down the pupils' confidence and stops them from trying that is the problem.

Expectations. I was not predicted high grades in primary or secondary school. I remember a teacher in secondary school that was limiting me to passes. I wanted to get distinctions but that is not what was expected by my teachers. This discouraged me but at the same time encouraged me to prove my teachers wrong. At first it demotivated me but then I used it as a tool to succeed and I did in the end. When I was in college, something that helped me was the arrival of a new Black teacher, teaching B-Tech. I related to her. When I was stressed out, I could confide in her. She would encourage me. She would ask me to keep going. She motivated me: she said things like, "you can do this." She helped me through college and I do not think I would have done as well if she was not there. As a teacher now, I set targets by looking at previous year data to tell me the level a pupil is performing at. This tells me what I am working with from the beginning. Thereafter my job is to determine how I can help each child improve. However, depending on past data is sometimes problematic. I remember having a boy starting in my class who was deemed average. As we progressed, I realised he was not average but very capable in his writing, maths and all the other subjects. I took it upon myself to move him up and now, he is in the top 2 pupils in my class, but if I had left him in the bottom sets, this would have continued to damage his confidence. This made me look at other pupils in the bottom sets and realise that a lot of them were capable. All they needed was a you can do it, encouragement and support and they could too move up. I have experienced this a lot. My pupils know that no matter where they are, I have very high expectations for them. I make them do their work again if it is below par and I have noticed that this has an impact on them and their work and even their motivation to do well.

Teaching Techniques. The lessons were teacher-led. I remember at university we did a lot of work on talk. Allowing children to talk in lessons. Giving them a chance to talk to one another while you teach. In my lessons, I encourage children to have a talking -partner. I encourage them to talk to their partner about what they like, dislike, think or they have Iearnt. I give the children the opportunity to be the teacher for 2 minutes and I discovered that this engaged them far more than when they just sat there quietly. What is more I found that this secured their performance and made my job easier because when they got back to their tables, they knew where to start and they just got on with their work independently. I would not say necessarily that Black children learn differently from White children but it helps if they are allowed to speak. This is because we as an African culture can be opinionated and used to voicing our beliefs. Muting a child in class causes them to shut down and disconnect from the lesson. This may then lead to behavioural problems. At the very beginning of my teaching, in the first 2 weeks: I thought this pupil was disruptive, naughty and just wanted to chat all the time. But then I realised that all she wanted to do was be heard and be allowed room to speak. As soon as I arranged this, her behaviour improved. Interestingly when I was at school, I felt that White pupils were given a chance to express themselves more than Black pupils. The other thing was that White pupils were given a bigger reading part if we were reading a book or when we were doing comprehension as a class. Pedagogy has the most impact on a child's performance.

Classroom Size. I remember having 30 pupils in my class. It was too many. Sometimes I did not get any of the teacher's attention. As a teacher, I feel that having less pupils is better. For example, in my class I have 31 pupils and it is quite difficult to fully support all of them. I do have a teaching assistant who has a lot to do outside of teaching. For example, she reads with the children. This is not the school's fault. There have been cuts in the budget. One of the problems is getting access to support teachers. Support teachers are crucial for pupils that need the one-to-one support. I think a suitable number would be 20. The teacher-pupil ratio changes based on where you live.

Classroom Set-up. KS1, I remember us being on the carpet a lot. KS2, I remember us sitting at square tables. I preferred KS1 because it was a lot more interactive. I felt closer to the teacher. We were all close together, telling stories. This helped with my concentration. The teacher had a pre-planned sitting arrangement. This worked for me so much that I adopted it in my teaching. This works because there are no arguments about seats. As long as it is fair and equal. Fairness is important to children. I have pupils from different ethnic background mix in class. I had a White pupil in my class who I think enjoyed mixing. In class I remember sitting at the back and was distracted lot. It made me feel disconnected from the class. This affected my behaviour as opposed to sitting in the front where the teacher watched you so you had to concentrate. As a teacher, I tend to put the children who get distracted closer to me and the children I know are capable of concentrating, I tend to put them towards the back. This works well because I am very close to the children that need the help. They can reach out if they need me and they are a bit cautious of their behaviour.

Teacher-Pupil Relationship. In secondary school it was harder to access teachers. If you have a question and it is not answered your work suffers. As a teacher, I tell my pupils that I have an open-door policy and I find that they just naturally come to me with anything. They will speak to me on the playground or on the street. As a Black pupil knowing that there is support, it encourages you to do well. I was closest to the Black teacher more than any other teachers in college. This is because I could relate to her. She understood me. It was amazing. I trusted her. Even when she knew that I was behind, she would still encourage and support me. I felt like: she was just like my parents. White teachers looked out for White pupils. I remember this teacher who if we were all behind on our homework, she would say I am not going to look at your work, but then she would say to some people, ok, let me have a quick look. Stuff like this discouraged me a lot and put me through unnecessary stress. What I would do is get the Black teacher to look through my work. Another example was when I nearly missed my university application deadline because this teacher was telling me she was not going to look at my work. This created unnecessary anxiety and pressure for me. I feel that the way to improve teacher-pupil relationships especially where the teacher is from a different background is by the teacher bringing themselves down to the level of the student and understanding them and where they come from. It is also important to listen to the pupil whether they are perfect or not. Continue to remind the pupils that their success is at the heart of the teachers' job. This is because I did not feel that my teachers wanted me to do well. I do not remember having specific lectures or seminars teaching me how to develop a relationship with the pupils and I did my teacher training recently. I believe pedagogy, what was taught and how it was taught including the teachers' implementation of the teaching was the most impactful to my academic performance because even when the curriculum changes the teacher still determines how they are going to deliver it.

Donna's Story

Representation. I did not like history. I felt as though I was not represented in the poems in English and Literature. For RE, the lessons focused on Catholicism because I went to a Catholic school. One of the students who was a Black Muslim sat there and said nothing throughout. In RE, we could have been taught about ancient religions. I could have identified more with this because of my culture. Furthermore, we could have been taught about Islam, or Judaism, to prepare us for the diverse world that we live in today. History was very much the British version. We covered slavery and everyone looked at me and I felt awkward. People looked to me as if I was the spokesperson for Black people. I was always tired of talking about this subject because it was not the nice part. The narrative was that slavery was in the United States and not Britain and the focus was on Britain's role as the abolitionists. It would have been important to learn about Britain's role in the slave trade and pre-colonial African history. We learnt about Egypt but I felt that this was always the go to when there are other countries in Africa with equally rich histories that we could have been taught about. I was a good student, always in sets 1 or 2. However the way slavery was taught demoralised me and destroyed any future ambitions in me studying history. Even now, I do not like talking about history, or historical events. I have a negative connotation towards it. I am interested in the modern stuff.

Streaming and Settings. I think sets are limiting but they can also be encouraging. I remember being moved down to set 3 in science. There was a lack of structure that was unlike sets 1 or 2. It was hard for me to focus and I knew I did not want to be in this set. I wanted to do better. What they did was divide us and we were given different papers. This was limiting. I wanted to move away from this and do the best paper I could and get the best possible mark. When I was in sets 1 and 2, I was encouraged to keep up with what my peers were achieving. It is almost like when you are at the top, the only way is down so there was the pressure to work hard and stay up. If I had a chance to design sets, I would look more at how people learn rather than their ability. Because the people in the lower sets weren't necessarily less intelligent but they learnt in a different way. We need to cater to people with different needs. "The stereotype is that people in the lower sets are unruly but it might be that they have individual needs". The majority of people in my school were White so you had both Black and White students in the bottom. The difference was that those at the top and bottom did not move sets except for those in the middle.

Expectations. I got all 5s in my SATs and that was the basis of expectations set for me. I am competitive as a person so I just want to do my best and I did not want to be seen as lazy. When I was put in bottom sets, it was like can you not see that I am better than this? I need to get back up.

Teaching Techniques. I think a lot of it was teacher-led but sometimes they would give the pupils a chance to speak. This was the structure but every class was different based on the subject. I enjoyed my physics teacher's style of teaching and I got an A* which surprised me. The teacher was a young White man and very urban. I felt like I could connect with him. We could have a conversation. He was that cool teacher that anyone could talk to". He used references relating to popular culture that I could connect with. He was still stern and you still felt that you had to do your homework. He provided the balance that I needed, unlike some classes where the teacher was either too friendly and lost control or too strict which constricted me from breathing. I also think that the styles lacking in discussion did not work for me because it felt like it was a chore.

Classroom Size. It was generally about 30 of us. This was ok but at the same time some students needed more attention than others and they became the focal point, taking away from everyone else. Because I got on with my work, I felt that the teacher ignored me, whereas other people who asked questions got the teacher's attention. In primary school, we did not have many Black students so we all mixed. In secondary school, I started to meet other African people and gravitated towards them and in sixth form, my friends were African because this is what I had missed out on in primary school. In primary school, it was not cool being African so hanging around my White friends was ok. In secondary school, I was more confident around my Black friends because we could share stories about our childhood and upbringing. We had a relationship. Today, the majority of my friends are Black because we identify in a similar way. I don't think not having many Black friends in primary school was a problem because I was tall and this and not my race was the focal point". In terms of race, I think a Muslim child going to school today will face similar difficulties as the Black children did. I think schools should emphasise that Black kids are just as human as everyone else.

Classroom Set-up. It was desks in rows. I sat at the back and there was a lack of teacher support: I got distracted and lost engagement as a consequence. At the back, there were pupils with behavioural problems and some bullied me because of my African heritage.

Teacher-Pupil Relationship. Once I left the classroom, I did not go back because I did not want to be seen as a disturbance. I wanted minimal interaction. I did ask questions in class if I did not understand something instead. I would not necessarily approach a teacher in the playground, maybe the form tutor. They did not teach me so I felt I could talk to them if I had any issues. There was also my PE teacher who I could talk to. It seemed to be that I approached teachers that were external to my academics. It was mainly because they could separate the classroom me from the playground me. I think pupils should have access so they can ask questions. Teachers should make themselves available but equally important is how they receive you. Information outside of the classroom should not be brought into the classroom to impact how they see you. It was for the fear of this that I did not approach teachers. I felt like some teachers were interested in me but others were there to do a job and go home. I was most impacted by pedagogy.

Danielle's Story

Representation. I came to this country and joined school at the end of year 9. I did the core subjects and would have liked to do more languages but you could only choose one so I took French. I was also interested in both geography and history but I could only choose one. The options were limiting. The history lessons could have encompassed more about the link between British imperialism and the rest of the world. This would have helped my peers understand my connection to this country. They covered a little bit about the civil rights movement and slavery. Being a student with English as an additional language, I had to work twice as hard. The teachers didn't understand my experience. They could have spoken to my family and had a better cultural awareness. This would have helped me integrate into the schooling quicker.

Streaming and Settings. For my O levels I was put in sets. First, I was put in the English as an additional language set and when the teachers realised I was doing all my work with ease, they moved me to the middle set. I was still doing better than the other kids here and they had no choice but to move me to the highest set. This was all due to my hard work. Sets can be helpful but it depends on how a teacher uses them. When I started, I was put in the English as an additional language class because of the stereotypes they had about me instead of assessing to find out what level I was at. Sets can be a self-fulfilling prophecy. If you say that children are not good enough, they may produce work to fit that level. However, sets can be beneficial to differentiate the support offered as long as they are flexible. Children should be assessed often to ensure they are moved up as soon as they are ready to avoid situations where they get bored.

Expectations. The expectations were low. Despite this, I did very well, I got A's and B's because I worked hard at my O-levels. But A-levels was a different ball game. You had to be creative and do research and without support or help you struggled. At the outset the teachers would have known that my dream was to be a doctor and as such they should have told me what the expectations were. Keep your marks above 85% in maths and sciences and if this was not the case, the teachers should have alerted me and supported me to get back on track but no one bothered to because they thought I was not good enough. This crushed me and my self-confidence. As a primary teacher, I engage with my pupils to check how well they are doing and if problems persist, I try working together with their parents or guardians. If the parents are struggling, I offer them help in whatever the subject is. We go through the curriculum and necessary materials so together we can help the child succeed. My teachers did not trust me. In my A-levels, my biology teacher made a comment that my use of language was not to the expected level to succeed in that class. Again, this shook my confidence and stayed with me.

Teaching Techniques. This was teacher-led. I would have liked to see more visuals and group work and interactive lessons. I should have had more chats with my teachers about my targets etc. Teaching style and social class should go hand in hand. If you are teaching children that have just come from a war zone, your style should accommodate the child's experiences. There should be cultural and language awareness so the teacher can connect and the kids can trust the teacher. The lack of connection negatively impacted my academic performance.

Classroom Size. We had about 28-30 pupils in the English as an additional language class. Here children were disruptive. I did not learn much from this class. When I was moved to the top set, classes were smaller and I was able to get some attention from the teacher. This was better.

Classroom Set-up. We sat in rows. I chose to sit at the front because I wanted to learn. For shy students, the teachers should place them in the front so they can access, engage and help them. In the bottom sets you chose where you wanted to sit and it was similar in the top sets. During my O-levels, I self-excluded because I did not want the kids to know about my background. I would go to the library. Newly arrived immigrant children should be paired up with other suitable children in the different subjects to help them integrate.

Teacher-Pupil Relationship. At the time, Labour had funded a lot of English as an additional language programmes. Under the care of social services, attempts should have been made to find a more suitable school for me. They should have ensured that the integration process worked and they should have had follow-ups. For example, I was assigned to English as an additional language class. Here students were sent to acquire language. The consideration was that I had just arrived from Uganda, they did not know what to do with me and just sent me there at lunch time. The pupils were at different levels in English. Coming from Uganda, an English-speaking country, I was different from say someone from a French speaking country but we were all lumped into one. Immigrants are all looked at as the same in English as an additional language class but they should be looked at independently. The school should have had an admissions policy to create an education plan for me. Engage with my parents. Sometimes I was behind with my work but I taught myself at home so I would catch up. This is because I came from a background that values education and this is why I succeeded. White pupils and Black pupils who understood the system would have had a better experience than the Black pupils born elsewhere. In their failure to engage, the teachers failed to understand that not all Black kids are the same and have different needs. Some kids were from Africa and others from the West Indies. Some were born here and others not. Some were working class and others not which meant we all had different needs. These were never met. On the other hand, White middle-class students in secondary school had better treatment. Teachers were sometimes racist and they did not know it. When you see that I am struggling and you think that I am aggressive or when I do not do my homework and you think that it is because Black people are lazy, then you are racist. The problem lies with the teacher training that does not take into consideration diversity and inclusions or the curriculum design that doesn't incorporate Black perspectives. I was doing sciences and none of the Black pupils made it into medical school. Maybe just one Somali boy who was super smart. We were all directed towards Biomedical sciences. The issue was that we did not have access both at school and at home. The White students had family or friends who worked in the medical profession that helped them with placements and could call in favours unlike us. They had help with their homework and projects and when it came to us, it was that we were lazy. The problem is you start to believe them and blame yourself. "I am lazy", even if you have been to numerous hospitals and no one will give you a job. The teacher relationship is very important.

Dolores' Story

Representation. My favourite subject was maths. One of the issues I had was that my teacher was not willing to help me. There weren't that many Black pupils in the higher sets and I realised that the teacher focused more on the White pupils. I think it was racist. I would constantly put my hand up but was ignored. She would come to me towards the end when there was not a lot of time left. I thought this was very unfair. She never even offered to help me out of class time even though I was willing and always asking. She would say she was busy. She could not even refer me to another teacher that could help. This happened to me a lot which made me think it was not a coincidence. As a result, I gave up, I would not ask questions or approach her. I ended up complaining to my mum and she got me private tuition to fill in the gaps. I think this teacher should have put her feelings and beliefs aside and helped me or refer me to someone else. In geography, the focus was on North America, Europe and a bit of Asia. We never learnt about Africa and I thought this was strange. It is geography: it is meant to cover the whole world. As a result, I lost interest because I was not being taught what I considered my part of the world. The funny thing is that when I was younger, I used to love talking about different countries. I knew all the African countries and capital cities off by heart. So now that I was learning geography, I expected to learn a few more things or at least be taught something that I was familiar with because I had come to this country when I was 10. The impact was that I started to lose myself. All I had was European and no Black.

Streaming and Settings. I was in sets for maths, English and science. I was in top sets for maths and English. I only managed to stay in the top set for maths because I had a private tutor. I think sets are good but I noticed that the top had White and Asian pupils, middle sets had a mixture and the bottom was mainly Black pupils. Sets were based on SATs assessments. It was very difficult to move from one set to another. Even if you got high marks and kept reminding the teacher, you were rarely moved up. The teacher would say, just keep working hard. The kids in the top sets had access to more challenging work which all kids should have a chance to look at and decide for themselves. If I were to design sets. I would assess pupils frequently to ensure they are in the right sets.

Expectations. I was set very low expectations. I remember going to the parents' evening with my mum and I noticed that they would always have lower targets than what I was achieving and I continued to achieve above this. I could not understand this. The teachers would say to my mum that we do not think that she is cut out for this subject. It did not make sense. I think this was racist. The impact was that I was driven to achieve even higher. Teachers should set expectations based on actual results and not what someone looks like.

Teaching Techniques. I remember doing a lot of group work. First the teacher would explain what we were expected to do. We would then go in groups and try to work out the answers. As a Black pupil, I enjoyed group work because it kind of forced everyone to communicate and get along to find the answers. It was kind of bonding in a way. I performed better with this style. Also, in my maths lessons where I felt that the teacher did not like me, my questions were answered because they were group and not individual questions.

Classroom Size. There were between 20-30 pupils in a class. I would have liked 15 because the teacher remains in control of the class and maybe then I as a Black pupil would have the opportunity to be seen and heard.

Classroom Set-up. The set up was in rows. I used to sit at the back and then I started to move to the front. We sat where ever we wanted. I sometimes chose to sit at the back because that was where my friends were. I mainly interacted with Black pupils. It was always segregated and, in some lessons, I could not see my friends so it was difficult. Sitting at the back was a problem because the teacher forgot about you. Which had a negative impact on my performance. The teachers should pre-arrange seats and mix up students.

Teacher-Pupil Relationship. Some teachers were really interested and did form a relationship with the pupils and I felt that I could trust them. This pushed me to do well. I was always in a positive mood in this class. I was not closed-off. The teachers created this environment. Because I had just come into the country, it was really important to feel welcomed by my teachers. Teachers should treat all pupils the same. They should have interest in everyone. I felt that other teachers were not approachable. When I had problems with my maths teacher, I approached another teacher who was Black. I remember talking to him about my experiences in the classroom and my mum talked to him as well. The Black teacher supported me and would explain things I had not understood in the lesson. Thanks to him I did well in maths. Schools should provide to the students and parents a list of teachers and timetable of when they are available to help. Teachers can make or break you.

Deborah's Story

Representation. I am currently working with children with special education needs. I normally work under a SENCO. I have been doing this for 10 years. While at school, I did not feel represented in the curriculum. As someone from a mixed-race background, I would have liked to see more about other races. When you are growing up, it is very important to learn about where you come from. For me, there was nothing about my identity. I found my identity from my family. Being mixed raced I know they do not cater to all, but in England we have such a diverse population and we should. I think not knowing where I come from had a negative impact on my confidence. This improved when I got older. I do remember being taught about Henry VIII. I would have liked to learn about the impact of other races in England. That would have been a nice thing for young people to learn because then they would know their role and contribution to this country. When I design my lessons, I use themes that children can relate to. This is not possible all the time but it helps when done. I remember once during a World War I and II lesson I was delivering to children who are not allowed into the main school. I played them some clips and asked how they thought the children at that time might have felt. I asked the pupils to put themselves in those children's shoes and write a letter to their family. We shared this amongst us. These pupils could all relate to this from personal experience and it was a memorable lesson.

Streaming and Settings. In secondary school they put us in sets in year 9 and they separated us and put us at different levels. I was in the middle sets for science and English and bottom for maths. Sets work both ways. Sometimes you can have a class at different levels, with some pupils progressing faster than others, then sets are good because you can cater to individual needs. Also, sets assist a teacher in knowing what level the children are at so that they know how to help. However, being in the lower set, in maths, sometimes made me feel less intelligent than my friends. This knocked my confidence and it is a vicious cycle. The rate of Black to White pupils in the bottom sets does change based on where you live. Sometimes you have more White children in the bottom. If the teacher labels them based on behaviour rather than performance then they may also end up in the bottom.

Expectations. The expectations depended on what I was confident in. Because I was not confident in maths, the expectations were low. In fact, I am still not confident in maths today. The teacher would assess you and separate you and tell you this is the highest you will get. This was out of order because when you feel that there is a limit then you think: what is the point in doing more and being a teenager, you think the whole world is against you anyway. As a teacher, my expectations are based on the individual and not the framework. I look at a pupil's past performance and check for progress to date because some children might have been working hard in the holidays.

Teaching Techniques. When I was younger, some lessons were practical. IT was practical but lessons like English and maths were not and I feel that core subjects are very important and should have been interactive. We just sat there and went through text books. This was wrong. As a child you should be given roles to play and interact. This would have been the best way. I try to make my lessons interactive but obviously we do follow the national curriculum and guidelines. But I also do my own thing. I use YouTube quite a lot. I will use interactive games so I keep the children intrigued. Some people will say that you cannot have them play games in an English lesson but if it teaches the kids phonics or how to construct sentences then I will have them in my lesson. I find that specific styles work for Black pupils and sometimes it depends on the parents. For me the way I handle the Black or mixed-race pupils will be different from how I will handle my White pupils. But I don't think all teachers have the Knack. They do not connect with or have the sort of relationship with the pupils to do this. This positively impacts the pupils' performance. There are pupils who this has totally changed their life whereas before I got there, they were being kicked out of school and actually within a term, I have changed their whole perspective on learning and they stay in school. The most important thing for teachers, especially if they are not the same heritage as these children, is to try and understand them firstly and try and build a relationship with them because no one wants to come to someone they do not like. A lot of the teachers need to know where these children have come from. Not only their country but where they live. For example, children whose parents are dependent on drugs, teachers have to sympathise with and help that child. For me, I do research around these different issues so I know how to handle the different children. I know you can't learn about everything but knowing a range of different cultures, backgrounds, societies in this day and age would help. Empathy will determine how a teacher handles a child and this determines how the child reacts and with support they will more than likely prosper. My relationship with my teachers depended on their teaching style. I remember my English teacher: I could not stand her. I could not stand how she spoke to us: I could not learn a thing whereas other pupils did. But as soon as we were put into sets in year 9 and I changed teachers, she was brilliant. I started to do better. The teacher spoke clearly, she was friendly, she could have a giggle. Yes, when you can have a bit of banter in class, children love it. Have a little bit of a joke and ask them to get their work done at the same time, they like that.

Classroom Size. When I was in school, there was 25 pupils in a class. I would say it is not good to have over 25 pupils because you will not be able to help all the children. You will have those that get help at home and the children that need a little bit more help from you. Teachers cannot teach 30 children. I do not think they can. The teacher-pupil ratio is significant to the performance of Black students. Extra curricula activities and support during out of school hours helps build a child's esteem and they will fare better. Even with higher numbers in a class they are more likely to follow compared to those that do not have similar resources which a lot of Black pupils or those from disadvantaged backgrounds do not.

Classroom Set-up. We sat in rows facing the teacher. In primary school they put you in a group of 4 per table. This was my favourite. I liked sitting at the back because I did not like people coming too close to me. Looking back this was not good for me because I was probably missing a lot of things and the teacher was too far to help me. If a teacher realises that I am not progressing from the back, they should move me to the front. It should be the teacher's responsibility. Being mixed race, sometimes you are trying to find your place so I sat with a mixture. My mum is Greek, my dad is Jamaican. You did not feel that you fit in on either side even though both sides really love you. Growing up you are always trying to find your space in society. So, it was a mixed group. I had a Turkish friend that I thought was related to me because my mum is Greek-Cypriot. I had a mixed Chinese and African friend as well. This positively impacted my performance. My Turkish friend had high expectations set for her from home and when we sat together in class, she always did her work and made sure it was neat which encouraged me to change my handwriting to match hers. Over the years this is still how I write. I was a high achiever and I remember sitting with a friend who sometimes struggled and I supported them which helped them in their GCSEs. The teachers in school did not do much to encourage this peer support. They just let it be and they still do to this day. The teacher could designate seats and over the week pupils could build a relationship and they could pull each other up.

Teacher-Pupil Relationship. My teachers were not as accessible and this maybe because of their work load. If I felt that I could approach my teachers for support I could have done even better. If you send teachers emails and they reply: if they have an open-door policy: if I am getting the feedback, the support and attention, I can only but succeed. Students should be able to access their teachers via email. There should be teacher timetables outside the classroom so pupils know when teachers are available. There could be drop-in centres, maybe at lunch time where kids could talk to someone. I think this would make a dramatic change. Pedagogy more than the curriculum is the most impactful on the academic performance of a Black pupil.

Delilah's Story

Representation. The curriculum did not represent me as a Black person. I would have liked to cover Africa, where we come from and a range of religions and worship. It was very much English based. We covered how England developed but not how it developed off the back of Africans. They brought up slavery and highlighted how we sold our own people rather than explain how the money from slavery was used to build the country. Geography did not cover the whole story. They did not talk about how the West divided up the African terrain and different communities were forced to combine. For example, some Ugandans and people from Rwanda ended up as one community. As a Black person I would have liked to know more about this. The way this was taught does not show a Black pupil who they are and their success as a people. It was limiting. Growing up I hesitated getting involved in some things because I was not sure that it was my place.

Streaming and Settings. I was in top sets in the core subjects. I think sets are good because pupils require different levels of help. However, it sometimes seemed that they were more reluctant to put certain people in certain sets. If you were Black, they would allow you in the top set but they constantly checked to make sure you could do the work. As opposed to the White pupils who they just left to get on with it. It was as though they did not trust that a Black pupil was good enough to be up there. We had to work twice as hard to prove that we had a place in that set. Constantly having to maintain your place is tiring. I was constantly picked to answer questions and I constantly worried about having the knowledge to answer. This actually reflected in my GCSEs because I did not get the expected results. I do not think White pupils suffered like me because they were looked at differently. They were good enough. I remember trying to join this school and they told my mum that I would not be able to get in. This secondary school was very sought after. It is strange when I look back because even though I was in top sets in primary school, the teacher told my mum that I would not be able to get into this secondary school but I did.

Expectations. The expectations set for me in primary school were low and I proved them wrong. It was the same for secondary school. I think expectations were set based on race for Black pupils and class for some White pupils. So regardless of your class as a Black pupil, the expectations were the same as a lower-class White pupil. This made me work harder. I do not know what the solution is.

Teaching Techniques. A lot of the teachers had a participative style. However, as a Black pupil, we were not as involved to the point where the teacher would be shocked if you gave a good answer. I liked the participative style but I think it would have been easier for me to just get my work and get on with it.

Classroom Size. We had 29-30 pupils. This was ok but I struggled with not having other Black pupils in my class. I felt that a smaller group would have been better to support. The size impacted my academic performance because they spent most of the time with those they wanted to focus on.

Classroom Set-up. We sat at desks in rows. I sat at the front. The seats were arranged by the teacher. I would have preferred to sit wherever I wanted because this would have been more comfortable. Sitting at the front put me under so much pressure. When it came to the questions, I knew that I was going to be one of the pupils asked. In the language classes this negatively affected my performance especially if I did not know the answer. This created doubt and it was in front of the entire classroom. I think the best setting would be at a round table with the teacher in the middle then everyone would have equal access,". The Black people stuck together and I think this was not good because we developed the mindset that we were separated. We could not share ideas and there was no growth. Teachers should make an attempt to mix up their pupils.

Teacher-Pupil Relationship. My teachers were accessible. This was good because you could get questions answered. I would have liked to see a bit more structured and regular meetings. This would have helped the teachers understand my progress. I think the teachers found it tricky relating to Black pupils. It was sometimes too friendly and it was not that they were interested in knowing about my culture or background. They should have tried to find out how my background impacted my academic performance so they could change how they approached me. The curriculum impacted my academic performance more than pedagogy.

Dale's Story

Representation. I did not feel that my culture was represented anywhere in the curriculum. As a Black man, I would have liked to see where we have come from over time because they teach you about the Tudors, they teach you about the English system and stuff but with the African history it is just slavery. Slavery was taught in a light-hearted way. As I researched slavery, I realised that we were not taught about the discrimination and how slaves were transferred to other countries. Back then I did not think much of it but as I grew older, I started to wonder whether this was really the history of my culture or the English perspective. I do not think it impacted my academic performance but maybe others.

Streaming and Settings. I was put in the middle sets in maths, English and science. This decreased my motivation because I felt less intelligent than the kids in the top sets which was not the case. I felt less worthy. I think it should have been mixed up. The support should be more in the lower sets but I experienced less support. The lower sets had 60% Black pupils compared to 30% Black pupils in the top sets. Back then I thought sets were determined on your results but I know they are determined on behaviour. That is how it was in my school. I am not against sets. If there are people that need support then that is fine but I think there should be a mixture and a group for those that would like to be supported that way. Sets were limiting because you were assigned either a higher or lower paper and you could not change this even if you wanted to take a higher paper.

Expectations. I was set low expectations but I would have liked a higher target to motivate me to work harder. Schools should not set low targets for pupils.

Teaching Techniques. It was mostly teacher-led but sometimes we would discuss. As a Black man, group work and talking to the teacher is better than just allocating work and asking pupils to get on with it. Peer support is crucial to academic performance.

Classroom Size. We had 30 pupils in a class with one teacher to help everyone. For me it would have been better if there were less people in the class because the more people there are in a class, the higher the number of White pupils, which means less support for Black pupils. An appropriate number could be 15-20 students.

Classroom Set-up. We sat at round tables and I liked this because we could talk in groups. I sat not far or near the teacher but somewhere in the middle. The seating arrangement was pre-planned by the teacher. Because I sat in the middle, I could get support and I could focus. In my class I felt that there was a divide between ethnic minorities and the White pupils. It puts you as a Black person in the wrong mindset.

Teacher-Pupil Relationship. My teachers were accessible but only during school hours. If I needed to see a teacher, I would ask to speak with them after the lesson. I only had 1 Black teacher. I felt that White pupils talked to the teachers more than Black or ethnic minority pupils. The relationship was purely teacher-pupil and nothing like where we could have a chat. It was always about the school work and no interest in me at all. This sort of a relationship limited my ability because all they were interested in were my grades but I did not really matter. It was demotivating. I would have preferred a very comfortable relationship where we could talk about anything. One that is not as professional and not just about work. Schools should set-up regular meetings where pupils can talk to their teachers and school should inform pupils that whenever they wanted to talk, a meeting could be set up. I don't think I would have walked up to the teachers outside of school. I think the teacher relationship impacted my performance the most.

Darcy's Story

Representation. As I am originally from Trinidad, I would have liked to learn about things that happened in the Caribbean. The slave trade and how we got to the Caribbean. I would have liked to learn about Black culture, but not only Black but Indian people because they also came as indentured labour to work on the plantations. This is rich history that should be taught. When I look at my son's work, I do not think that what is covered today during Black history month is sufficient. They talk briefly about Black historical figures like Rosa Parks and Nelson Mandela, but I think there is more to African and Caribbean culture that should be included. They just do this to cover their backs and say I have taught Black history but ethically they have not. Why do we not learn about Africa before the Europeans invaded? How did African culture then change to Caribbean culture? Black people in the Caribbean did not just drop from the trees. We came from somewhere. How about the Arabs? It is important to see Black in the school so Black pupils do not feel alone. Another area is the lack of Black books which really hurts Black kids. This causes them to lose themselves and their self-esteem because they are around a culture that tells them that Black is worthless and has not contributed to the country. If I was born here, I think, I would have lost myself too. What has protected my son is that he goes to Trinidad in the summer and for two weeks he goes to school with his cousins where they are taught our history. As a result, he learns about Black culture. So, when he goes to school here, the little they cover in Black history month he already knows.

Streaming and Settings. I think sets are terrible because it made us think we were not as intelligent. All children should be treated equally regardless of their ability. There is racism in the education system and if the teacher does not like a child, they will use sets to bring them down. Every teacher has their favourite. For example, my son had a teacher in year 4 who was not very good. When I approached her to talk about what my son was struggling with, she shrugged me off and said she did not have time. In class she would put my son aside and thankfully the teaching assistant noticed and told me what was going on. I went to the head and reported this. My son was then given the support he needed. In the case of the teacher, I think she was 1) lazy and 2) I know that she attended a grammar school herself so maybe she didn't not know how to handle children in a state school.

Expectations. The expectations were low when I went to school. This was racist. Black people are stereotyped to be lazy and so this is what they thought. Also, because some Black parents just accepted whatever, we were expected to just accept to work at the levels they allocated us. I say to my child you can achieve whatever you put your mind to. Dr. Eric Williams who was the first Black president of Trinidad and Tobago was deaf but he excelled so can you. I did not settle with the school's targets. I worked even harder to succeed.

Teaching Techniques. It was a teacher-led style with the teacher at the front and we listened. For my son I think it is a mixture of teacher and the pupils get involved. I think it is better because my son has a chance to say what he thinks.

Classroom Size. There were 30 pupils in a class and I thought this was poor because we were all at different levels but were expected to cope. It is still 30 kids in the class for my son but they have a teaching assistant sometimes. There should be less than 20 kids in a class.

Classroom Set-up. We sat in rows and I sat at the back. This was because I was shy. It hurt me because I lost focus sometimes. Teachers should keep shy students at the front so they can support them. Which did not happen.

Teacher-Pupil Relationship. I would have liked to have Black teachers at my school because they can relate to and support Black kids a lot better. In my son's school, there are no Black teachers. I think as a girl it would have been nice to have a Black female teacher teach me about being a strong Black woman to supplement what my parents were doing. The same applies to Black boys. My son looks up to President Obama and he says, Mum, if he can be president, then maybe I can be president too. Little Black children seeing Black teachers says to them that maybe they can be teachers too. Some Black parents are not as supportive of their children with schooling because they are scared of the pushback if they raise issues. They do not get the support from the English education system to support their own children. So, they just leave it to the school. Whatever the teacher says, whether good or bad, they do not question. Some Black parents have the I am grateful that my child goes to this school attitude. Schools should regularly update the parents with their children's progress and advise them of the suitable materials the children could use while at home so they can catch up. Teachers should share with the parents where they as a school need support and the home and school should work together to support the child. Teachers were not as accessible while I was at school and I did not approach them partly because I was shy and scared of them. How teachers are with you affects you the most.

Dean's Story

Representation. I was nowhere in the subjects I was taught. The boys in the books were blond, blue eyed. How could I find any interest in only reading books that had White people in them? I hated the slavery lesson. I could feel all those White kids looking at me. In fact, I remember the kids saying I looked like some of the kids we had seen in the lesson. It was horrifying. We do not include Black people and when we do, it is in a derogatory way.

Streaming and Settings. I was in the bottom sets. We had very little support and there was no way we were going to be moving up. There was nothing for me to aspire to.

Expectations. As a Black person, no one expects you to be worth anything. The problem was that my parents believed the school. They believed I did not do well because I was lazy and they did not think that the teachers could have been racist.

Teaching Techniques. It was a teacher-led style. We sat there and listened. The lessons were very boring: I fell asleep in some of them. Teachers should involve the kids in the teaching.

Classroom Size. We had 30 pupils in a class. I do not think the size of a classroom matters. It is all about the teachers and their attitude. You could have a small class but if the teachers are racist then they will not support Black kids.

Classroom Set-up. We sat at tables in columns. I sat at the back because I did not want to be in class. My friends sat at the back with me. We chose where we sat and did very little work. I did not get very good grades. Kids from different backgrounds did not mix much and this was not encouraged either.

Teacher-Pupil Relationship. Teachers should treat everyone the same. I sat at the back to avoid the teachers. We did not have a relationship. I did not feel that they wanted to know me. Teachers were very strict. This had a negative impact on my performance. The teacher relationship had the biggest impact on me as a person.

Daisy's Story

Representation. I think at my school the curriculum is inclusive. We try and draw from different backgrounds in the topics. For example, we celebrate all different cultures, we have assemblies to do with Black history. We do not study traditional history. We study Africa, America and all the different continents. We learn songs in other languages. At my school we study about history all through the year and not just in Black history month but I think in London, we have historically focused on this in Black history month. At primary school, we focus on poetry and picture books based in Africa. Slavery has a very sensitive side so we celebrate the positives out of that when teaching it. It is more after KS2 that the 11-year-olds go into much detail but it is a very sensitive issue to teach. Some of the positives from slavery that we look at include the contributions, the survivors and their strength and how it came about. I do not know if the kids at the lower stage would know about slavery. At KS2 they use picture books to learn about slavery. At our school, we have children from so many countries in Africa. We do encourage these children to share their background and where they come from. We have a map of all countries that they can refer to. I think again it varies from school to school but our school is pretty good at that.

Streaming and Settings. Historically, they do think that Black children underperform but I think it depends on the cohorts. For example, in some of our classes at the moment, the pupil premium, who are those that are considered disadvantaged, there are no gaps. There does not seem to be that trend in our school. If we do see a gap, we put an intervention in. We have small groups. I think that children of different abilities perform better in mixed groups because the high achievers can support the low achievers and vice versa. If you have a class where they are all low achievers then there is nothing for them to aim at but if you have a great child who works hard and is really competitive, the other kids will really work to strive and get up to them. Kids can bounce off of each other. In KS2, that is the first time that kids are graded. In my school there are no gaps. We have had really bright Black kids who have gone on to get scholarships. Maybe the divide gets bigger as they get to secondary school. I do not know the reason why that maybe but, in my experience, there has not been a divide. With us, we grade the kids in year 2 when they do the SATs and then at KS2. Again, the curriculum has changed in the past 2 years. It used to be levels, if you were in year 6 and were bright, you would be in level 5 but now it has changed. We have 3 systems, we look at expected level, above or you are working below it. So, these are wordings we use to grade kids. Again, among the pupil premium kids, there is not a gap. Movement in sets is very flexible because we are a very small school. Infact in year 6 we have 1 class. So, the kids are not moved to a different room but we have tables, a top table but even within that we have flexibility and kids move on when they are ready. We have introduced this thing into maths called maths monastery where everyone starts at the fluency level, where it is just the simple calculations. Some kids will be working at that level where you cannot access the higher-level problem-solving thinking but still within the class and others at a higher level. The teacher will differentiate by giving out the different work. Those kids that are able, the teacher will ask them to move on to something else and they might have a bit of guidance. So, within lessons, there is much flexibility and movement around what the kids are doing and what they are able to do.

Expectations. Within our school, we have a behaviour policy so it does not matter what colour or background: the expectation is that you try and do your best at everything. Our expectation is the same in academics. Our expectations for children with English as an additional language is to get them as confident even when they cannot speak properly. At the start, we find that those that do not have the language might be at a higher level in other subjects and obviously language is very important. It is different for different subjects. Again, because all our classes are mixed ability, with a new pupil who has English as an additional language, we try and get to know them. If we feel that language is the only thing that is letting them down, then we have an intervention in place to support them with their language. It is trying to know them first and determine where to put them.

Teaching Techniques. We use visuals. In maths we use a lot of concrete methods for their counting. We get them moving around. They act out and use a lot of repetition. A good teacher, regardless of their background you have got to try and incorporate different styles and try to get the point across. I would not say that Black pupils learn different from White pupils because we have quite a lot of White pupils who come in and actually their language is not as strong and it is because maybe their parents do not speak to them much at home. It is all about seeing kids as individuals and seeing how they learn.

Classroom Size. Typically, we have 30 kids with one teacher and a teaching assistant. Personally, I think between 20-25 is more beneficial for the kids. The impact of teacher-pupil ratio on Black kids depends on how many other Black kids there are in the class. But again, with White kids as well, 20-25 is a better number. You may have some really bright kids mixed in with those that struggle then obviously it is a huge job for the teacher to do. Teaching assistants could be a solution to reducing the ratios but not every teacher has a TA. It depends again on the class. Some classes will have a TA because they have children with special education needs. So, it depends on the needs of the class whether or not they get a TA but I think having the extra helps. If we did not have TAs, it would be extremely hard for teachers.

Classroom Set-up. At our school there is a lot of flexibility with the teacher. It is up to the teacher how they want to set it up. Every class has a book corner, an interactive white board and a creative area. We celebrate the kids work more so than formative text so there will be displays to show what the kids have achieved. Classroom setup does not matter, or what the child's race is, as long as you inspire them. Lower down the classes the seat arrangement is a free flow and the kids can choose whichever areas they want to go to based on what interests them. As they get older it is more formal learning and they are expected to sit at their table. With the free flow, the kids mix and maybe at primary school the kids just do not notice these things whereas maybe it becomes more present, more apparent when they get older. But from day 1 when you see them, they just interact, you don't see the White kids going there and the Black kids going there. There is no difference. With the seating arrangement and mixing I find that the Black kids are outspoken. They want to be heard. They want to voice their opinion. I think it depends on the child, their character and so many other variables.

Teacher-Pupil Relationship. We have an open-door policy at our school. The kids can go to their teacher whenever they want to. As teachers we are usually in our classrooms so kids can come up to us when they have issues. I think teachers are equally approachable for both Black and White kids in my school. I hope that I come across equal to all of them and they can approach me regardless of their background. I try and support them all in whatever way I can. I think this is also part of our behaviour policy. It is in the code of conduct so it is part of our job to have that openness. We give out emails to parents or carers for access but we are not allowed to give these to children. The children know where to find the adult if they need to. My relationship with Black and White pupils is not different. Sometimes as a teacher you do develop different relationships with different kids. Some maybe more challenging than others. You still have to be professional and sometimes you can't help but you have a different relationship with different kids. I do not think this is necessarily a divide between Black and White. It depends on the character of the kids and character of the teacher. There are some kids who like adult attention regardless of their background. You can see that at play time they chat away to the adults and do not have much time for the kids and vice versa. There are kids who are extremely shy and they find it hard to approach the adult. When children first arrive, they are buddied up with a child in the older year group to make them feel more welcome and show them around. Before they came to the school, they will have filled out an application form which tells us about their background, where they come from and who they live with. In the early years we do encourage the kids to share if they want to. The teacher gets the kids into circle activities so they do not feel isolated. You ask every child the same question. Where they come from, what they like doing and that kind of thing. Over time you develop a relationship. In my school, we are encouraged by our head to interact with the kids during play and lunch time when it is less structured. As teachers we are not necessarily encouraged to attend community events as a way to learn more about our pupils but within school, we have our own fair where we encourage parents and other people to get involved. They can bring in their skills or help where ever they can. They can bring in their own food and we share. That sort of brings the different background together but that only happens once or twice a year like Christmas and summer. As a teacher, the job is demanding so I do not believe you would last if your motivation is purely financial. It is not a 9-5 job and you do not just switch off. The hours that teachers put in out of school hours is crazy. So, you have got to love your job to do it. When it gets to teacher training, I think inclusion and diversity awareness could be something that could be improved upon. There should be more staff training during inset time to learn about the different cultures. Having been at the school for 15 years I have built some good relationships but if you are new, there is so much to learn to do with different cultures. You are not given that time when you start teaching. Straight away you have to prepare the lessons. You are encouraged to make them as diverse as possible and make sure they are culturally adaptable. Another thing that could be done to help would be a better transition from primary to secondary school. This might help close the gap. At our school we work very closely with our year 6 pupils before they go to secondary school. We try and have a good form of communication with the new school. At primary school, they get to know one teacher and when they get to secondary school, they have different teachers. This is unfair. Maybe the kids in primary school should be exposed to and experience more than 1 teacher. This might improve the transition. I think pedagogy has the most impact on pupil performance.

Dante's Story

Representation. I learnt the normal maths, English, science and some optional subjects. I did not feel the subjects represented me. Schools should make more of an effort to engage with their Black students. They should know more about the culture so the students can engage with the curriculum. Then they might see an improvement in performance. We could learn about Black music, beliefs, religions etc.

Streaming and Settings. I was put in sets in the core subjects. I was in the top sets. I think sets are good at categorising pupils but they are not 100% reliable. The problem is that sets separate students and rely entirely on assessment but not ability at a given time. I noticed that there were less Black students in the top sets.

Expectations. The school set me low expectations. Some people were encouraged to work harder and others not. Schools should reach out to the students and find out what the pupils are really like and what they are capable of.

Teaching Techniques. They would often have a teaching assistant and sometimes we learnt using PowerPoint. This method was good for me. The style was participative and it allowed me to engage with the lesson and remember things more easily. Teachers could have spent some time explaining things more clearly.

Classroom Size. There were 30 pupils to a teacher and an assistant. This made it difficult to divide time equally between students. Especially since some needed more time than others.

Classroom Set-up. The set up was in rows. However, my preference would have been round tables so I could interact with other students easily. I sat next to the teacher. This was easier to have eye contact and remain engaged. Sometimes it was a pre-planned seating arrangement and other times not. I preferred having the choice because then I could always sit at the front. The majority of the Black pupils sat at the back and it was easier for the teacher not to pay attention to them. Teachers just carried on as if this was ok. I noticed that Black students from the lower sets hang out together because there were more of them whereas the ones in the higher sets were more likely to mix with other races. Being the one Black student in the top sets impacted my behaviour and how I viewed myself. This is because if your circle of friends is White people then it is more likely to influence you. For example, the Black students in the top sets spoke differently from the ones in the bottom sets.

Teacher-Pupil Relationship. My teachers were accessible. You could arrange to meet with them in their office after school. I had more White teachers than Black. I think access is important because students can gain confidence from knowing that they can get the help they need. This directly impacts performance. I had a positive relationship because I was a top student. Teachers generally treated the top student better.

Debra's Story

Representation. I do not think that the curriculum represented me. It was mostly White culture. I would have liked to see diversity but then, maybe I grew up in a different era. In the 70s and early 80s, racism was still rife. Had they introduced more of the Black culture way of living, a lot of false information would have been erased. Maybe we could all have understood that we are equal. When we touched on Black culture, it was mainly slavery. They portrayed something that was incorrect. If I was a teacher, I would deliver the slavery topic to show that it was morally wrong instead of making it seem normal which is what was done. This impacted my love for geography and history and I dropped both subjects as soon as I could.

Streaming and Settings. I was put in the top sets for English and French and middle for maths. We were pushed more at the top and for the middle I wanted to get out because I would look at some people and think why do I want to be here. I do not think sets are particularly right because they tend to favour the brighter children. They get more teacher attention which really should be going to the lower sets. I went to a majority White school and so the top and bottom sets had both Black and White students.

Expectations. I was predicted high grades because of my academic work. This pushed me to work harder. Having said that, I was pushed from home because my father had very high expectations. However, I think higher expectations should be based on what you can achieve. Just because my dad was good at sciences, does not mean that I am too. I was not good at sciences. I was good at arts. This had more of an impact than what I was predicted at a school. If I was to design sets, I would look at ability and provide individual help for the kids that need it.

Teaching Techniques. The style was participative. This was a suitable style for me. I just went with the flow.

Classroom Size. There were about 30-35 of us. This was suitable.

Classroom Set-up. We sat in rows. I was happy with this arrangement. To start with we sat anywhere but to be honest, in those days I was naughty and so the teacher sat me next to people I particularly did not like. I did not like it at the time but looking back on it, it was good for me. I mixed with White pupils but unfortunately, I was bullied. I had to turn into the bully to defend myself. I would fight them. This got me into a lot of trouble in school and at home. I was not really happy at school. It was not fair that I had to get into trouble. At times I felt that it was not dealt with properly. They turned a blind eye to what was going on. When I reported the White kids, I was accused of telling tales.

Teacher-Pupil Relationship. Teachers were not accessible in those days unless it was a detention or something. I found it easy to raise my hand and ask a question in class but I would not go to the teacher's office if I had a question. I think this was because we did not have that sort of relationship. Also, you were not encouraged to. Teachers just stayed in the staff room with the door shut. Looking back on it now, it did not really impact my academic performance but it would have been of great help. The teachers should have let pupils know when they were available. I think things have changed today because of technology. It is easier to get in touch with someone by email, phone or messaging. I did not have a good relationship with my teachers because I was scared of them. I tended not to ask questions which then led to a not good performance compared to the ones I found approachable. A lot of teachers were strict and overbearing. Some teachers were interested and some had the I cannot be bothered attitude. I did not perform well in their subject. As a Black pupil, the teacher pedagogical approach had the most significant impact on my academic performance because there is nothing like a good teacher, showing encouragement and looking over what you are doing in class.

Derek's Story

Representation. I remember learning English, maths, science and drawing. I do not remember any of the books we read. It was not interesting to me. I do not read for fun. Only when I have to. I would rather listen to music. I do not know why I do not enjoy reading. I do not remember learning anything about my culture maybe slavery. As a Black boy that was born in this country, the slavery lesson was embarrassing. I saw all these naked people in chains and at first, I was not sure what was happening but I now know they were being sold. I assumed all the other children who were mostly White saw me like this. I go back to the Gambia quite often and I would have liked to see some of the beaches in my geography. I was not present in what they taught me and as a result I was not present at all.

Streaming and Settings. I was in the bottom sets for English, maths and science and I did not move up. The classes were disruptive. There was a lot of us who needed help. I do not think the teachers could cope. I did the lower papers and I found them difficult. I enjoyed football so they let me out to play a lot of the time. I think dividing us into groups was good because we needed help but they should have given the support to go along with this but that did not seem to come. They just left us to work things out on our own. I think they left us to fail, they did not care: we were Black. The sets were bad because you got in with the wrong crowd sometimes and I think because of this, I was never going to get better in my work.

Expectations. They set me low targets. In the lower sets we sat all the easy papers. I think teachers think that all Black people are capable of is playing football and singing. There was a lot of Black kids in these activities. I think this is also the case today. When you look at football or the music industry. I did not enjoy the work so I spent a lot of time on the playground. I think teachers should always encourage kids to do better.

Teaching Techniques. The teacher stood at the chalk board and we listened. I do not remember getting involved, I just listened or call it daydreaming. I could not wait to get to playtime. I think teachers should involve the kids in the teaching. They should ask the kids what they think a lot more or how they want to be taught. My teachers were very strict and old fashioned they would not have done this. We were scared of them. This also contributed to me not liking the lessons. It is interesting because my parents were strict so this should have worked but I think the difference is my parents loved me but the teachers were not interested.

Classroom Size. Maybe 30 pupils or more. The classes were in a mess. No one knew what to do. The teacher just continued at the front.

We did not learn anything. I think classes should be smaller for the kids that need the help. Maybe 15 kids per class and I think the teachers should be trained to know how to assist these kids. This also led to my loss of interest in learning.

Classroom Set-up. We sat at tables in rows. I did not think this was good or bad. I did not know another way. I sat at the back. This was my choice because I did not want to answer any questions. I did not know the answers. I think sitting at the back was not good for my concentration and because I chose the seat, I remember sitting next to my friends all the time and all we talked about was football. We did not think about the lesson at all. This was not good for our performance.

Teacher-Pupil Relationship. I do not remember talking to any teachers. Maybe when we were bad. But outside the class, I liked the P.E. teacher. He liked me. I was good at football. I wish I had felt the same way for my lessons maybe I would have done better. In a way sport was good for me and this is the area I work in today. I think teachers should have been a little more interested in the Black kids. They should have moved around the class and maybe asked to look at my work. They would have known I needed help. They could have offered to see me outside of the lesson. This is because I was scared to put my hand up and say I was finding things difficult in front of my friends. I think the teacher relationship affected me the most. If all my teachers had been like my P.E. teacher then maybe I could be a teacher now.

Shared Narrative Meaning

During the collective analyses, I identified the shared narrative meaning across the stories and highlighted recurring themes and subthemes. As I put the stories next to each other and constructed their similarities and differences, the lack of worth of the Black pupils to the teachers echoed throughout their stories. The lack of representation in the curriculum and a positive teacher-pupil relationship were resonating threads in the stories of the Black pupils. Ideas around teaching about the African and Afro-Caribbean culture and the African continent connected these diverse stories together. The value of education was something that was cultivated into some participants from home and some parents did not know how the English education system worked. Table 7 shows the subthemes (from the previous section) under the themes curriculum and pedagogy.

Themes	Sub-themes	Number of participants
Curriculum	I felt the curriculum did not represent me	(20)
	I was placed in lower sets	(18)
	Those for whom expectations were low	(15)
Pedagogy	Those that experienced teacher-led style of teaching	(16)
	Those in a class of more than 30 pupils	(17)
	Those who sat in rows and at the back	(12)
	Those who experienced a positive teacher-pupil relationship	(5)

Table 7
Themes and sub-themes

Chapter 4
Discussion and Implications

Key Findings

The findings from this study will inform researchers, the DfE, Local Authorities, educators, administrators, Black parents and the Black community who play a role in the education of Black pupils in England. It broadens our understanding of how Black pupils experienced schooling in England between 1950-2000. In addition, we learn how these previous experiences impact the participants as parents and teachers today. As well as the participants life in general. What is more, the study elevates the often overlooked, underrepresented group of people within research in education. Education is the bedrock of someone's future. If we get it wrong the impact is long lasting, affecting someone's career, social mobility and family. Some may end up involved in the criminal justice system and the cycle continues for the next generation.

Curriculum

"The national curriculum states that every child should be taught the folk ways and morals that represent them ethnically and culturally." Dylan.

The majority of participants testified to being taught the best that has been thought and said by White people. It was a Eurocentric curriculum that promoted British values, successes and history with no space for African or Afro-Caribbean faces, voices or being. A significant number remember learning about the Tudors, in particular Henry VIII. This is important because it helps all pupils understand present day religion, Britain and the international community. Equally as important was these now adults learning about the ancient African kingdoms and civilisations: Imperial Britain and Britain's role in slavery and later colonisation: and benefits Britain accrued from Imperialism in relation to today.

"As a Black boy that was born in this country, the slavery lesson was embarrassing. I saw all these naked people in chains and at first, I was not sure what was happening but I now know they were being sold. I assumed all the other children who were mostly White saw me like this." Derek.

"They brought up slavery and highlighted how we sold our own people rather than explain how the money from slavery was used to build the country." Delilah.

Representation. The majority remember that infamous slavery lesson in history which has tormented and traumatised some to this day. This was an opportunity for these Black pupils to learn about their history: How we come to find Black people around the globe, in Europe, Asia, North and South America. In addition, these Black pupils would have learnt how their ancestors contributed to civilisation and in particular, Great Britain. This will help a White child understand why they have a Black child sitting next to them in the classroom. In addition, it will prevent Black children from growing up with a distorted idea of who they are. It will build their self-esteem and confidence which trickles into every part of their lives and the next generation.

"Geography did not cover the whole story. They did not talk about how the West divided up the African terrain and different communities were forced to combine. For example, some Ugandans and people from Rwanda ended up as one community." Delilah.

"In primary school, in geography, we looked at Western cities and towns and Africa was portrayed as a village," Devine.

"In geography, the focus was on North America, Europe and a bit of Asia. We never learnt about Africa and I thought this was strange. It is geography: it is meant to cover the whole world. As a result, I lost interest because I was not being taught what I considered my part of the world." Dolores.

Once again geography lessons omitted the Afrocentric perspective, Africa and Black pupils. The continent of Africa has vast amounts of natural resources, not to mention some of the largest, deepest, longest and highest: parks, lakes, rivers, and mountains in the world. This is information that is important, not just for Black pupils but White as they learn about the world. Today we talk about environmental issues but how is it possible that we can teach kids about hurricanes in the Atlantic, Gulf of Mexico and Eastern Pacific Ocean without teaching them about the African Easterly Jet winds from the Sahara Desert that majorly influence weather across the Western Hemisphere? Their knowledge will be distorted. These participants lost interest in a very important subject and the continent lost potential Black researchers.

"I did not see characters or language that I could identify with. If English was your first language you did not need to understand the structure. However, this makes it difficult to understand the structure and how other languages work. This especially affected my ability to learn other languages like French when I was at school." Dawn.

"I was expelled at 15 and I started to attend Black History lessons. There weren't many students that attended these lessons. For me, it was during these lessons that I was taught about my African and Caribbean history, I was Introduced to famous writers like J. A. Rogers: something

that has stayed with me." Dylan.

"I was nowhere in the subjects I was taught. The boys in the books were blond, blue eyed. How could I find any interest in only reading books that had White people in them." Dean.

The participants did not identify with the books the teachers used during the lesson. There were no Black characters or books by Black authors. This tells the kids that only White people have had something to say that is worth putting down on paper. This destroys a four year old Black child's love for reading. What is more, it impacts their ability to comprehend and understand other subjects compared to children that enjoy reading. This is because English language is the thread that links all the subjects in the curriculum. Overall, a lack of representation in the curriculum meant that pupils could not identify with what was taught and their performance was poor.

Streaming and Sets. The majority of participants were placed in lower sets. They were graded in year 2, KS1 when they did their SATs and then again at KS2. This was used as a basis to determine which set they were placed into. The KS2 assessments were used to determine sets at secondary school. The majority of participants were put in sets for the core subjects. The experience was demotivating with no prospects of being moved up. The participants reported experiencing disruptive behaviour. Sets were limiting because they were assigned to lower-level exams. Some even reported seeing more Black than White pupils in the bottom sets, as well as children with special education needs. There was a lack of personalised support and teacher interest in the pupils in the bottom sets. It was suggested that mixed groups were better because they enabled pupils to help one another and work in teams. Overall, sets are necessary because pupils work at different levels, but they should not be based on the teacher's prejudices or pupil's behaviour but put in place to provide personalised support.

"I was in top sets for English. I loved books but due to family difficulties, I missed a lot of school and I was moved down to the bottom sets where people struggled to spell their names or had a mild learning disability like dyslexia. I felt like this was unfair because missing school was out of my control as a child." Dawn.

Expectations. For the majority of participants, teacher expectations were low. This was either because pupils spoke English as an additional language or because of racism. Some participants used this as a form of motivation to work hard and prove the teachers wrong. On the other hand, some saw no point in trying. Their teacher was such a significant voice at that early stage in the pupil's life that whatever they said was true and stayed with them to this day. Some participants testified to being set very high standards at home, so it did not matter what anyone thought of them: they were going to achieve and very highly. Overall, low expectations were equated with poor performance.

"The school had low expectations of me because I had just come from another country and I had an accent. They thought I was not up-to-standard compared to someone that had grown up in the system. I was depressed. It knocks you and has a huge impact on your life. My academics suffered and I missed out. Your school days are supposed to be the happiest. But when that is not right, the foundation is weak and the future is bleak. I wish I had one-to-one support from my teachers, maybe during out of hours. I can't blame the teachers because this is probably how they were taught. Maybe they did not know how to deal with students." Dorothy.

"The expectations depended on what I was confident in. Because I was not confident in maths, the expectations were low. In fact, I am still not confident in maths today. The teacher would assess you and separate you and tell you this is the highest you will get. This was out of order because when you feel that there is a limit then you think: what is the point in doing more and being a teenager? You think the whole world is against you anyway. As a teacher, my expectations are based on the individual and not the framework. I would look at their past performance and check for progress to date because some children might have been working in the holidays." Deborah.

Pedagogy

Teaching Techniques. The majority of participants experienced a teacher-led style of teaching. The teacher stood at the front of the classroom and delivered, while the students, sat down listened and answered questions when they were asked to. This style did not work for some participants and they described losing interest. It also meant that some pupils who were shy did not get involved or were lost along the way. This is why it is important to get the pupils talking, as was suggested by a participant. On the other hand, some participants explained how they worked in groups or were engaged by their teachers, a style they enjoyed and use as teachers themselves. Corporal punishment in schools was allowed at the time. It was because of this that some participants were terrified of their teachers. This then negatively affected the entire school experience and academic performance of some participants. However, some participants described an urban pedagogical approach where the teacher made references to popular culture that pupils could connect with, a style that yielded an A* in physics to a participant's surprise.

"Mine was predominantly a teacher-led style. The teacher sat at the board, giving you information and you copied this and occasionally did some group work. Teachers were allowed to punish or cane so I was very frightened of them. I would sit quietly, watch the board and listen to the teacher. I am a visual learner. I like to see things. I think other ways of learning are better other than chalk and blackboard. For instance, a more varied approach where we could come up with ideas ourselves in groups. It would have been better if we had a chance to think before the teacher gave us the information and role play to get the message across. Science should have been much more hands-on rather than sitting down and listening to a teacher. Science should be more feeling rather than listening. I didn't do very well at school. I had a very difficult childhood. I missed a lot of school. Teachers were always angry with me and they shouted at me a lot. There was a lot of bullying going on and I didn't have the voice to say "you are bullying me" so that made me more reluctant to go to school. I would hope that teachers are more understanding these days." Dawn.

"The teaching styles that I enjoyed are the ones I have used as a teacher. It is effective to involve the students in what they are learning in one way or another. As a student I enjoyed the engaging style of Mr. Cleo and Mr. Samuel, the only Black teachers in the school. Learning is about who teaches you and how they teach you. I enjoy involving students into what they are learning. They do little projects that we include in lessons. They will bring in examples from say, YouTube or a newspaper. I prepare my students for whatever the lesson is about. For me, it is about the engagement." Dylan.

"The lessons were teacher-led. I remember at university we did a lot of work on talk. Allowing children to talk in lessons. Giving them a chance to talk to one another while you teach. In my lessons, I encourage children to have a talking -partner. I encourage them to talk to their partner about what they like, dislike, think or they have learnt. I give the children the opportunity to be the teacher for 2 minutes and I discovered that this engaged them far more than when they just sat there quietly. What is more I found that this secures their performance and makes my job easier because when they get back to their tables, they know where to start and they just get on with their work independently. I would not say necessarily that Black children learn differently from White children but it helps if they are allowed to speak. This is because we as an African culture can be opinionated and used to voicing our beliefs. Muting a child in class causes them to shut down and disconnect from the lesson. This may then lead to behavioural problems. At the very beginning of my teaching, in the first 2 weeks: I thought this pupil was disruptive, naughty and just wanted to chat all the time but then I realised that all she wanted to do was be heard and be allowed room to speak. As soon as I arranged this, her behaviour improved. Interestingly when I was at school, I felt that White pupils were given a chance to express themselves more than Black pupils. The other thing was that White pupils were given a bigger reading part if we were reading a book or when we were doing comprehension as a class. Pedagogy has the most impact on a child's performance." Devine.

Classroom Size. The majority of participants were in a class of 30. This made it difficult for the teacher to attend to all pupils equally. One participant explained that a high number of pupils in a class equated to Black pupils getting less attention. On the other hand, the size of a classroom is irrelevant because the teacher controls the class and if they are racist, then they will discriminate against Black pupils. Some participants used this as an opportunity to hide away and not answer questions in class. Teaching assistants were suggested as a solution, or a class of between 15-20 pupils. However, as a participant stated, cuts in school budgets compromise the availability of teaching assistants. Some participants testified to having smaller classes, which gave them easier access to the teacher. However, this restricted the generation of ideas and group work.

"Typically, we have 30 kids with one teacher and a teaching assistant. Personally, I think between 20-25 is more beneficial for the kids. The impact of teacher-pupil ratio on Black kids depends on how many other Black kids are in the class. But again, with White kids as well, 20-25 is a better number. You may have some really bright kids mixed in with those that struggle then obviously it is a huge job for the teacher to do. Teaching assistants could be a solution to reducing the ratios but not every teacher has a TA. It depends again on the class. Some classes will *have a TA because they have children with special education needs. So, it depends on the needs of the class whether or not they get a TA but I think having the extra helps. If we did not have TAs, it would be extremely hard for teachers." Daisy.*

"There were anywhere upwards of 15 in a class and maybe a few more in economics. With the maths and physics lessons, it was not so much the numbers, but that you had quite a range of abilities within that. You had people trying to work hard to get an E-grade and on the other end, people like myself who were trying to get an A-grade. When you have people of that breadth of ability in a class it is a challenge for the teacher to teach the material at the right level. This did not affect my performance because I learnt to go away and fill in the gaps to the level of detail that I wanted to cover, but it did require me to do that to deliver." David.

Classroom Set-up. The majority of participants sat at tables that were arranged in rows and columns. This was a good arrangement if a participant was sat at the front because they could easily access the teacher. However, some reported that sitting at the front put unnecessary pressure on them to get all the questions the teacher directed at them right. For those participants who were shy, sitting in rows at the back meant that the teacher left them behind, which negatively affected their academic performance. Some participants reported sitting at round tables which was a good arrangement because they had access to the teacher and peers and it facilitated better group discussions. More than half chose to sit at the back. They were distracted and this negatively affected their academic performance. The teachers had pre-planned seating arrangements and, in some cases, participants reported not liking this at the time but in hindsight realised that it helped them focus in lessons. Interestingly enough, some would have liked the opportunity to choose their seat so they sat at the front, away from the other Black pupils. In the lower sets, Black pupils interacted with other Black pupils but in the top sets they mixed with pupils from other ethnic backgrounds and some participants reported being bullied.

"We sat at tables in rows. I did not think this was good or bad. I did not know another way. I sat at the back. This was my choice because I did not want to answer any questions. I did not know the answers. I think sitting at the back was not good for my concentration and because I chose this seat, I remember sitting next to my friends all the time and all we talked about was football. We did not think about the lesson at all. This was not good for our performance." Derek.

"We sat in rows. I was happy with this arrangement. To start with we sat anywhere but to be honest, in those days I was naughty and so the teacher sat me next to people I particularly did not like. I did not like it at the time but looking back on it, it was good for me. I mixed with White

pupils but unfortunately, I was bullied. I had to turn into the bully to defend myself. I would fight them. This got me into a lot of trouble in school and at home. I was not really happy at school. It was not fair that I had to get into trouble. At times I felt that it was not dealt with properly. They turned a blind eye to what was going on. When I reported the White kids, I was accused of telling tales." Debra.

Teacher-Pupil Relationship. For the majority of participants, a relationship with their teacher did not exist, or it was poor. Either because the participants were intimidated by the teachers or the teachers were not interested in them. The implications were that participants did the work on their own, they were tutored out of school or simply failed in their exams. Some participants recall that one Black teacher that changed the course of their life. This Black teacher as in Freire's words became the custodian of knowledge, therapist and preacher. However, one Black teacher cannot support all the Black pupils in the school and carry out his day job at the same time. Some participants found it more difficult to access their teachers in secondary than in primary school and they could not have questions answered as a result. The problem was compounded for the participants that did the sciences because they did not have someone in the family working in the field. Therefore, they could not get the help outside of school. Teacher access was linked to various factors including a teacher's heavy workload, a lack of interest in Black pupils and technological development with availability of emails. However, participants pointed out that teachers should have an open-door policy where a pupil can just walk in for help or a chat. Furthermore, teachers should be accessible during out of school hours and they should get involved in the community so they can learn more about the lives of the pupils they teach. A participant highlighted the fact that their school holds summer fairs twice a year and gets parents involved this way. As much as this brings the school and community together, it is very much controlled by the school and may limit who is involved from the local community. Access is crucial because it gives the pupils the confidence in what they are doing and could help create a positive teacher-pupil relationship.

"I don't remember accessing a teacher, because I found them intimidating and frightening. A teacher bullied me to a point that other students stood up to defend me. If I didn't put my hand up, he would scream in my face and he would do the same if I got the answer wrong. As soon as lessons finished, I would just disappear and go home. That particular teacher behaved that way towards me because he didn't have control of the class or the respect of the students. I think he wanted to make an example of me: There were incidents where police were involved. Teachers had abused a Black child who refused to take her clothes off to do PE: this was in the papers. I don't recall having a relationship with any teacher: I would come in and leave quietly. I tried not to draw attention to myself.

It massively impacted me. I left school with no qualifications. I didn't have a good relationship with any teachers. They weren't interested in me as an individual and I didn't spend any time at school but I love learning and I knew that I had the capacity. When I left school, I went to college and did my nursing training and a nursing degree. I carried on doing things. I think everyone has the ability and teachers just have to encourage and support the pupils to achieve to their potential. They need to find out what and where problems are and help. Pedagogy most impacted my academic performance." Dawn.

"The teachers were quite friendly. I was vocal in class. I was also the one who would make the jokes. This helped me. I did well at school. I was never muted and never realised that my voice was irritating until I got older. The teachers made me feel like that. I think all students should have equal access. My brother had a different experience to me. He really struggled. There were phone calls home. He did not have behavioural issues as such but he struggled. There were a lot of things put in place for him. He was not vocal. My mum was vocal for him. I was kind of naughty. I was always talking when I should not have been talking. School is a very structured place. Okay I will tell you what happened in my first school. Why I was moved. I was in an assembly. I was giggling with my friend and the head teacher said, "stop talking", first time, second time and third time he moved me to the front and I was still giggling and looking back at my friend. So, he stood me up, shook me and said, "will you shut up" and told me to sit down. I sat down. I went home and did not say anything and my cousin said, did you tell your mum what happened. I said no. She said you did not tell her that he shook you. I said no. My mum overheard and said, he did what? While I was sitting outside the head's office a teacher came up to me and asked what I was doing and I said my mum is in there talking to the headmaster. She said oh is this about what happened in the assembly? I said yes. So, it was evidenced that it happened but somehow, he got off and continued to be a head teacher and I moved schools. This was in year 3. But this followed me in my record and am not sure how it impacted me. On looking back, I was talking because that was who I am. My mum said that from a very young age, I would just go up to people and chat. Even now I get home and I will be talking to people and my partner will say, "can you stop talking to strangers." As an adult I can understand how frustrating it must have been for the headmaster but I was incredibly young. As a teacher, if I had that little me, I would have taken it as my obligation to understand all the personalities in the room and mould my style accordingly. In primary school the children are young and sometimes will not be able to read the signals which can differ in secondary school. This whole situation did not impact me but my brother who loved my old school. He hated the new school and resented me for a while. He missed his Black friends. I think the solution is at teacher training. For example, Teach First are looking for people who went to a good university, got a good degree and so on, to go into their

programme. This is because they are about education, but personally I do not think recruitment is done for the right reasons. It is well and good to say we train people to teach but if the desire is not there, it would be very naive for us to think that every teacher is there because they love the profession. I think that is where the problem is. Teachers have to be passionate about wanting to work with young people and wanting to make them better regardless of their background. If you do not have this from the beginning of the teacher training, then it is going to be impossible after you qualify. Teach First is a very good programme if you want to become a leader. They give you a good salary but that is an incentive that is completely removed from the child. Children have to be at the centre of recruitment and why we get into teaching and not the other way around. I remember my personal statement, when I wanted to become a teacher, made the panel cry because there was so much love and passion in there. In every job I have done, the young person continues to be at the centre. Sorry, if a teacher does not have that, no unconscious bias training is going to correct this. I am very suspicious. I have seen teachers who love their subject but do not love the children. I think we need to find a happy medium. Teachers have got to make a conscious decision to get interested in the kids. The curriculum does not work for most students regardless of race because it is very much designed for the top maybe 20%. The curriculum is not fit for purpose and does not prepare people with the skills for work. Therefore, the relationship with your teacher is more crucial because they determine how you are going to digest the knowledge. They can make the difference in a child's life. I was that type of teacher. I would get kids that did not like the previous lesson because the teacher was not interested in them. It would normally be the older teachers because they do not like change. My way was, you can do it and a lot of them did well. I remember teachers for good and bad reasons and there is no in between. I remember the teacher who helped me with English at my GCSE and I went on to do English. I remember my maths teacher who moved me from the middle set into the top because I got 70% and I was able to do the higher paper. I remember that teacher because he saw what I was capable of. He believed in me. A good teacher is the most important thing," Doris.

All in all, underachievement may be the logical outcome for Black pupils because of the physical cost incurred as they attempt to acquire success. Alongside this are other factors including the phenomenon at-risk, which has been adopted to blame pupils for both systematic neglect and the failure of schools to provide a decent education for Black pupils.

Comparison to Previous Literature

Curriculum

Representation. Some participants were keen to learn about how Black people end up in Great Britain; and the question should be, why is this not taught? It is deliberate, a grand conspiracy to erase Black history because it contradicts what is known today. Fryer (2018) notes that the majority of Black people who came to England prior to the 20th century were brought as slaves and they were very young. In 1507, there were reports of a solitary Black musician who lived in London and was employed by Henry VIII. Over forty years later, in 1555, while attempting to break the Portuguese monopoly in the lucrative West African trade, John Lok brought to England, five African slaves from Shama, Ghana with the intention to teach them English so they could go back to Ghana and act as interpreters. From 1570 onwards, African slaves were brought to England in the capacity of household servants, prostitutes and court entertainers. In 1577, four Africans travelled with Sir Francis Drake on a mission to circumnavigate the globe. This was followed by one hundred and thirty-five Africans who were shipped aboard a single engineering ship to Bristol in 1590 (Olusoga 2016).

17th century. For the first half of the seventeenth century England's Black population remained very small. Then in the 1650's the numbers begun to rise steadily with the increased demand for sugar by both the elite and poor in England. In the1670s, West Indian planters' children, along with their Black attendants came to England for their education. In 1680, the planters in St. Kitts (England's first successful Caribbean colony) requested that the Lords of trade in London provided Black slaves to cultivate the plantations. This was to ensure that supply matched the high demand for sugar, tobacco, rice and rum.

18th century. Lord Chief Mansfield estimated that there were 20,000 Black people in England. A number that was to increase by over thousand because of the Black loyalists from North America who had exchanged the life of a slave for that of a starving beggar on the streets of London. The estimates were based on parish lists, baptismal and marriage registers as well as criminal and sales contracts. In the mid-1800s, Black activists including Olaudah Equiano (the chief Black spokesman of Britain's Black community), Ignatius Sancho and Ottobah Cugoano setup a movement demanding Black freedom from slavery through covert means, resistance and fighting. The activists were supported by the working and urban poor who themselves were suffering under the ruling classes of the day. Up until the third quarter of the 1800s, young Black slaves were brought to England as household servants by the planters. More young Black slaves were brought to England by the officers of slave-ships and sold privately to rich families or by public sale. Over the next century, other slaves were brought by government officials, army and navy returning from service abroad. Some Africans came to England as electricians, plumbers and seamen recruited to take the place of English crew members who had died or deserted on the African coast. 1786 saw the rise of the Black poor, these were ex-low-wage soldiers, seafarers and plantation workers who did not fit easily into the Poor Law welfare strategies of the period and as such a special Committee for the Relief of the Black Poor was set up and this laid plans for the settlement of Blacks in Sierra Leone, West Africa.

19th century. In the early 19th century, more groups of Black soldiers and seamen were displaced after the Napoleonic wars and some settled in London. The slave trade was abolished in 1834 and as a result, the number of Black people in England steadily declined. During the mid-19th century there were restrictions on African immigration and later there was a build-up of small groups of Black dockside communities in towns such as Canning Town, Liverpool and Cardiff. These communities were as a direct result of the new shipping links that were established with the Caribbean and West Africa. One of the most important Black people of this era was John Edmonstone a slave who gained his freedom and became a scientific researcher with skills of taxidermy (stuffing animals after they have died). He later became a lecturer at Edinburgh university, where he taught Charles Darwin who developed work on the evolution of mankind. Another significant Black person of this era was Mary Seacole a Jamaican who came, over to England in 1854. Seacole requested to go to help wounded soldiers who were fighting in the Crimean War (1853-1856) but was rejected by the War Office. She raised the money herself and travelled to Balaclava, Ukraine where she looked after British soldiers who had been injured. A statue of Seacole was built outside St Thomas' hospital in London in 2016. Again, pupils are not taught about Mary Seacole, only Florence Nightingale.

20th century. This era saw an influx of African students, people from sports and business as well as Caribbean students and professionals pursuing careers in medicine, politics and activism. On 22 June 1948, four hundred and ninety-two Jamaicans came from the Empire Windrush to England after a call for workers to help rebuild England after WW II. Some worked on the railways, some as labourers, electricians, administrators, plumbers and coach builders. Ten years after the Windrush, there were about 125,000 Black people making a mark with two out of every five born in England. Between 1960 and 1981, there was a succession of laws limiting Black people from entering the UK and there were struggles against racism and intolerance for Blacks. One of the leading Black people of this era is, Sir Learie Constantine, a Welfare Officer in the RAF who was refused service in a London hotel: he sued and won damages. In 1975, David Pitt became the first Black peer member in the house of Lords and this was followed by four Black Members of Parliament (MPs) (Diane Abbott, Paul Boateng, Bernie Grant and Keith Vaz) elected in 1987, six in 1992 and nine in 1997. Olive Morris was a civil rights activist who tirelessly campaigned for the rights of Black people in South London and Manchester. Olive Morris, Stella Dadzie and Gail Lewis founded the Organisation of Women of African and Asian Descent (OWAAD) and contributed an enormous amount to Black communities across the country. In 2013, Malorie Blackman was the first Black person to take on the role of Children's Laureate. Malorie's ambition is to make reading irresistible for children, by encouraging them to explore a range of literature, from short stories to graphic novels. she is also the author of the best-selling Noughts & Crosses series. In 2019, Bernardine Evaristo became the first Black woman to win the Booker Prize, a revolutionary landmark for Britain.

The participants were taught about Britain the abolitionists but as one of them suggested, there needs to be a balance. Pupils should also be taught about the European slave trade. The European slave trade was composed of the Transatlantic slave trade and the Indian ocean slave trade. The Transatlantic slave trade was the trade in captured and enslaved West and West Central Africans who were shipped across the Atlantic Ocean to the Americas between the 16th and 19th centuries. Whereas the Indian ocean slave trade was the trade in Africans who were captured on the coast of East Africa and shipped to the European-owned plantations in Mauritius, Reunion, Seychelles and the Americas via the Cape of Good Hope and Zanzibar on the clove plantations under Arab supervision. By slaves I mean the Africans who were captured and shipped to various other parts of the world to live and work as the property of Europeans. Slave trade refers to the transactions between the European buyers on the coast of Africa, or port of embarkation and European buyers at ports in other parts of the world. For the captured Africans the process was not trade, it was a form of social violence which included warfare, trickery, banditry and kidnapping (Rodney 1972). In the early eighteenth century, twenty-one million people were captured in Africa, seven million of whom were brought into domestic slavery, nine million were transported to the New World and five million suffered death within a year of capture.

All European countries except Russia stole, raped, murdered and exploited Africa and Africans in the interest of European capitalism. The European slave trade was the principal foundation of Britain's riches and the main spring of the machine which set every wheel in motion (Fryer 2018). Britain was the world's top slave trader, responsible for about more than half of the Atlantic slave trade. Britain supplied over 4,000 slaves a year to South and Central America, the Spanish West Indies, Mexico and Florida. The first ever recorded voyage took place in

September 1700 when the Liverpool Merchants delivered 220 slaves to Barbados. The triangular trade was advantageous because there was no money exchanged but arms, textiles and wine shipped from Europe to Africa: slaves shipped from Africa to Americas: and sugar, spices, molasses, rum and tobacco shipped from Americas to Europe.

British slave merchants netted profits of approximately £12,000,000 on the 2,500,000 Africans they bought and sold. Some of these profits were invested in land and houses and profitable trade links with Russia, India and China. The profits also financed the British Industrial Revolution and were instrumental in the rise of British capitalism. Textiles were manufactured in Lancashire: iron (making brass rods and cutlery) was manufactured in Birmingham: copper (making rods and manillas) was manufactured in Swansea: and other products (such as, gun powder, glass, spirits and tobacco) were manufactured in Bristol, Warrington, St Helens and Flintshire. All these products were bartered for slaves on the African coast.

According to Olusoga (2016), every brick in the cities of Bristol and Liverpool was cemented with an African slave's blood. Slavery transformed Bristol and Liverpool from mere fishing ports to great world ports. Bristol was built on the trade in slaves and the trade in slave-produced sugar. Liverpool was built from the trade in slaves and the trade in slave-produced cotton. London was heavily involved in the slave trade. London and the Bank of the West Indies which is now Bank of England, were the chief financiers of the entire slave trade system. The London merchants made profits on imported sugar, commission and earned interest from lending money to planters who bought plantations and slaves. The cycle was made up of the merchant capitalists who sold slaves to the planters, the slaves who produced the sugar, the industrial capitalists who supplied the manufactured goods with which the slaves were bought and the bankers and commission agents who lent money to all of them.

The slave trade was always very closely connected with local Government and it was tolerably well represented in Parliament too. Several of these 18th century merchants became aldermen. Of the 101 Liverpool merchants that traded in African slaves, 12 were or became mayors for at least 35 years between 1700 to 1820. In 1766, the Gentleman's Magazine calculated that there were upwards of forty MPs who were West Indian planters, or the descendants of the planters or those linked to slave trade (Fryer 2018). The Miles family were a Bristol success. William Miles became a leading sugar refiner, alderman and a leading local banker. His son Philip John Miles, another slave trader, died and left behind wealth of more than £1,000,000 from compensation of slaves in Jamaica and Trinidad amongst other things. Thomas Johnson the founder of modern-day Liverpool was mayor in: 1695, again mayor from

1701 to 1723 and knighted in 1708. The Cunliffe family were another success in Liverpool. Foster Cunliffe, Liverpool's leading merchant, was said to be Britain's biggest businessman. He was mayor in 1716, 1729 and 1735. Foster's son Ellis was an MP for Liverpool for 12 years between 1755 to 1767 and was made a Baronet. Foster's sister married Charles Pole who held the other Liverpool seat between 1756 to 1761. The Heywood family, brothers Arthur and Benjamin, made fortunes in the slave trade such that when Benjamin died in 1796, he left legacies of several thousand pounds and real estate and on the death of Benjamin's son Nathaniel in 1815, left behind £50,000 in legacies and Arthur Heywood Sons & Co. which was absorbed by Bank of Liverpool, then Martin's bank and later absorbed by Barclays bank. Another funded noble family of London was that of Henry Lascelles. He collected sugar duty on behalf of the Government and got rich from bribery and commission earning himself enough money to buy a seat in the House of Commons. This cost him £13,000. Lascelles sat for Northallerton from 1745-52 and on his retirement, his older son Edwin took over and on Lascelles' death, Edwin inherited £284,000 and annuities of £166,666. The slave trade further bolstered Lancaster, Whitehaven, Portsmouth, Chester, Preston, Poulton le-Fylde, Plymouth, Exeter, Dartmouth and Glasgow.

Towards the end of the eighteenth century, the struggle for the abolition of the slave trade was in full force. Upon the abolition, slave owners were compensated with approximately £20,000,000, while the slaves and their descendants received nothing. As a result of the European slave trade, Africa and Africans suffered ethnic fragmentation, depopulation, loss of labour and received no compensation (Fryer 2018).

The participants were taught about terrains in Europe and the Americas. Knowing that there is an abundance of resources from all corners of Africa, the participants would have liked to be taught about these. What is more, the participants were interested in learning about the role of the West in re-drawing the borders and creating new communities in Africa during the eighteenth century. Lovejoy (1989) reported that the European slave trade increased the degree of ethnic fragmentation in Africa. This resulted in social conflict and the development of mistrust which led to the long-term, systematic underdevelopment of many African economies. Furthermore, the slave trade helped shape the ethnic landscape that the colonial powers encountered in Africa. This landscape played a role in the partitioning of Africa, at the Berlin conference 1884/85.

The books used in class and recommended for home reading by the teachers were White centred. Perry (1971) states that the absence of a proportion of society falsifies literature. Consequently, Black pupils feel worthless, as they associate the lack of Black literature to only White people having done any thinking, feeling and achieving that is worth setting down. This creates self-hatred for the Black pupils and teaches White pupils racism. English teachers build foundations: if they teach literature without Black writers then they are saying to their pupils "lets read about what White people do and say." In addition, the lack of Black literature denies Black pupils the heroic representatives and principles that are associated with a sense of self-pride. They are denied a beauty of one's self example thereby causing them to grow up with a distorted self-image.

The inclusion of Black literature, makes Black pupils feel recognised and understood. It helps Black pupils connect the literature to their day to day lives, which enhances their engagement with the reading process because they feel that school and teachers respect and value them and that education is for them too. For White pupils, the inclusion of Black literature makes them aware that there are perspectives and ways to do things other than their own. White pupils build an understanding and respect for other cultures and this gives them a chance to examine racism. Black literature can add value to the language arts curriculum and it is crucial in stimulating reading in younger Black children because children receive the majority of their messages through pictures.

In addition, Boles (2006) warns us of the Above Excellent Syndrome, where nothing in regards to Black people is acceptable unless it is super-superior. However, while we search for extraordinary Black literature, we omit some of the most relevant writing which compounds the already existing problem of the shortage of Black literature.

"Whenever I am approached by my colleagues regarding the possibility of including black literature in the curriculum, I am asked if we should only include the very best of black literature, which it should be for all literature but is only brought up in relation to black literature".

However, Boles (2006) warns that sometimes teachers are overwhelmed by the prospect of having to find and evaluate Black literature as their intentions are not to offend anyone, but they might do so by accidentally selecting and sharing inappropriate literature. They might assume that the literature is worthwhile because it has non-White characters or themes and is cited in well-known journals. As pointed out by the participants, a teacher's day is demanding enough without having to add more demands to it. However worthwhile, this may seem impossible.

Streaming and Sets. Following the DfE's changes to the National Curriculum in 2014, most primary schools changed how they assess a pupil's attainment and progress from year 1-6. It changed from levels to a four-tier system. A pupil is either working towards, at, above or below the expected standard for their age. This is problematic as Dylan points out that some children are a year younger than their peers depending on the month they were born. Therefore, it is unrealistic that they are graded the same as someone older than them. What is more, some Black children who, having recently emigrated to England, join school and are put in classes with children below or above their age so the current assessment system would not be applicable. Similar to the participants, Wright (1986) found that streaming was not entirely based on ability and that the system worked more against Black pupils. There were fewer Black pupils in band A: something that was not related to capability but the lack of opportunity. In the same way, Burgess & Greaves (2013) criticized tests for being culturally biased against some groups and because of stereotypes, individuals were categorised into certain groups. A teacher created prototypes to make conscious or unconscious judgements about future pupils of the same group. This way some teachers were able to predict pupils' performance based on their ethnic group.

Wright (1986) recommended within-class streaming because it was proved to provide a benefit of three months additional progress for all pupils except those at lower levels. On average, pupils in sets made slightly less progress than those taught in mixed ability classes and the results showed that streaming had a minor negative impact for low to mid-range attaining pupils compared to a minor positive impact for higher attaining pupils. According to the Education Endowment Foundation (2021), streaming is not an effective way to reduce the attainment gap and is related to low self-esteem and confidence. This in the long-term has negative effects on the attitudes and engagement of low attaining pupils. Likewise, Harlen and Malcom (1999) concluded that there was no evidence to show improved attainment either through within-class or year group ability streaming. It had a positive effect in mathematics in primary school unlike in secondary school. Furthermore, it was found that teachers treated mixed ability setting as low-attainment groups and used inappropriate teaching methods.

Demie (2018) found that Black pupils were entered into lower tier exams which resulted in disengagement, poor academic performance and this educationally disadvantaged pupils in the long run. The pupils either ended up excluded: they did not progress to higher education: joined a gang, were involved in a stop and search: went to prison: were detained in a mental health facility: were unemployed or suffered from poverty. In addition, Coard (1971) found that a disproportionate number of West Indian children were placed in educationally sub-normal schools based on discriminatory IQ tests and assessment procedures which portrayed cultural and class bias, without taking into account issues around emotional disturbance experienced by immigrant children. Teachers believed that these children were physically larger than their White counterparts and deemed them threatening and more difficult to handle. Black children are lively and their liveliness gets them in trouble because teachers fear liveliness and school likes silence. To control them, teachers placed the pupils in disciplinary units called *sin bins*.

Expectations. Similar to this study, Coard (1971), Wright (1986) & Pumphrey and Verma (1990) found that teachers generally have low expectations of Black pupils and these attitudes negatively influence their academic careers. Racism is a major contributor to the poor academic performance of Black pupils. Haynes et al. (2006) quoted a teacher saying that, "there is no good reason why African Caribbean pupils underachieve, but the Blackness that leads to the failure." According to Mac an Ghaill (1988), when assessing English as an additional language, pupils, specifically speakers of Black British English or other languages, were labelled as less able because of the form of language they used. Teachers assume that they share the same language with their pupils, but they usually operate within a dominant form of language that pupils do not have equal access to. In this context, language can operate as part of cultural capital (Gonzalez 1984).

The participants stated that their teachers' expectations of them were low and that this was the case for their children. However, the DfE (2014) clearly states that teachers should set high expectations for every pupil. Teachers have an even greater obligation to pupils from disadvantaged backgrounds and they should use appropriate assessment to set targets which are deliberately ambitious. Teachers are required to take into account their duties under equal opportunities legislation to ensure that there are no barriers to any pupils' achieving. Pupils should be able to study the full national curriculum with support with any potential areas of difficulty identified and addressed at the outset. Also, teachers are required to take into account the needs of pupils whose first language is not English. They should monitor their progress taking into account the pupil's age, length of time in this country, previous educational experience and ability in other languages. Teachers should support these pupils to develop their English so they can take part in all subjects.

Pedagogy

Teaching Techniques. The participants described experiencing the teacher-led style which was similar to Freire (2017)'s banking concept. The participants were the have-nots, empty containers that were to be filled with and store information. They were the oppressed, welfare recipients. While the teachers, the haves who knew it all, dictated and controlled the have-nots. As testified by some participants, the school environment enforced the behaviour of silence, passivity and a feeling of inferiority. Similarly, Thompson (1980) described the function of schools as that of taming, subduing, chastening, demoralizing with the aim to render the children of the poor: honest, obedient, courteous, industrious, submissive and orderly. This style created a static, one-way system where information was not questioned and the pupils did not actively participate in organising it. Tharp and Gallimore (1988) agree that one-sidedness hinders pupil's ability to learn, narrate, explain, question and ultimately challenge the teacher. Furthermore, Alexander (2008), recommends talk as an effective tool for cultural and pedagogical intervention in human development. The teacher-led style is troubling. It gives teachers so much power over the pupil. As testified by the participants, a teacher who said, you can do this, motivated them to succeed at college, whereas the teacher who said the participant was not good at maths instilled a lack of confidence in them in maths which has gone on to affect how they teach the subject. The power structure also led to a participant's exclusion from school because he questioned the teachers.

Some participants described enjoying the participative style. This is similar to what Freire (2017) describes as true education: The student and teacher both exchanging perspectives and experiences and learning from one another. This gives the teacher the opportunity to assess the pupil's level of knowledge (Alexander 2008) and helps the teacher rid themselves of their false consciousness and prejudices. What is more, learning and knowledge could be acquired from outside school (Illich 1971). The participants testified to this by learning about their history from the Black community and family.

Some of the participants identified a lack of diversity and inclusion in teacher training programmes and a curriculum design that didn't incorporate Black perspectives as an issue. In the same way, Ladson-Billings (2000) criticizes teacher preparation for failing to equip teachers to effectively teach African American students. The teacher training focuses on individual courses and diverse field experiences to satisfy legislation instead of equipping teachers to meet the needs of diverse learners. Billings recommended situated pedagogies where teachers match the school and home experiences of Black pupils to ensure specific aspects of the Black culture are addressed. This helps teachers avoid generalisation. In addition, teachers could adopt an Autobiographical pedagogy that is personal and cultural in nature. This will allow Black pupils to speak as subjects with their own voice, representing themselves and their stories from their own perspective.

Classroom Size. Large classroom sizes had a detrimental effect on the academic performance of the participants and some reported that this is still the case today for their students and/or children. The findings of Goldstein and Blatchford (1998) testify to this. They reported a greater negative impact on the performance of Black pupils compared to their White peers in mathematics and reading in classes of 30 pupils and above. The DfE (2011) report also recommended a reduction in reception class size from 25 to 15 citing better literacy outcomes for pupils from deprived backgrounds. Finn and Achilles (1999) also argued for smaller classes. These were beneficial across all subjects for both boys and girls because teachers spent less time managing the class and more time instructing. Smaller classes also promoted greater interaction between pupils from different ethnic backgrounds and fostered better teacher-pupil interactions.

Classroom Set-up. In this study, the seating plan was mainly at tables, in rows and arranged by the teacher. Bicard et al (2012), agrees with this, stating that student seating is one of the easiest and most cost-effective classroom management tactics available to teachers to eliminate behavioural problems without the need for consequence intervention. However, Bicard acknowledges that offering pupils the choice to select their seats is ethically responsible and may be an important component of classroom management as well. A pre-planned seating arrangement, in rows led to better behaviour but when pupils selected their seats, there was disruptive behaviour which impacted completion of school work. Similar to the participants' stories, Gest and Rodkin (2011), found that teachers used seating plans to promote friendships ties, separate pupils that posed behavioural problems and to accommodate pupils that were shy in a classroom. Some teachers reported taking extra care and even being protective of those who were shy and timid and disliking pupils that caused problems or were bullies.

According to Minchen (2007), a pupil's position in the classroom could impact their attainment, the overall retainment of newly learned material and behaviour unless they were sitting in the front and centre of the classroom. It should be noted that moving a pupil who is struggling to the front has positive effects, but on the contrary it may be counterproductive if they are sat next to a pupil who is mutually distractive. Minchen found that pre-planned seating arrangements required careful planning with one bearing in mind pupil behaviour and the need to manage disruptions. Placing a pupil in a particular place always displaces another pupil, possibly to the back. There is a need to frequently rotate pupils other than those with SEN because it eradicates cliques which are counterproductive to good performance. This also helps stronger pupils by keeping them out of the poorer producing sections of the room and weaker pupils by moving them to higher performing sections. For balance, Minchen recommended that teachers reserve hot sits in the classroom designated for certain pupils who needed extra help. Alternatively, teachers could empower pupils by asking them to organise a regular rotation plan by themselves.

Teacher-Pupil Relationship. Similar to this study, Murray and Malmgren (2005) found that a positive teacher-pupil relationship in high-poverty urban schools could be inhibited by a number of barriers.

It was reported that teachers in under-funded schools that serve a high number of pupils from lower social economic backgrounds, struggled to manage basic routines. They received little administrative support and were implicitly or explicitly blamed for pupils' low attainment. As a result, teachers were frustrated and they felt hopeless. Teachers were short of time, energy and resources to develop and sustain meaningful and effective relationships with high-risk pupils. This was traced back to the shortage of teachers: recruitment of under qualified teachers and teaching assistants: teaching assistants who ended up performing the teacher's duties: and teachers being overloaded with work that should be done by two teachers.

All participants except one cited pedagogy, in particular the teacher-pupil relationship, as most significant to their academic performance. Wilkins (2014) agrees with them. In his study he found that teachers viewed a teacher-pupil relationship as central to all aspects of teaching. As a result, teachers developed good relationships with students primarily because they saw such relationships as serving instructionally beneficial purposes. Wilkins also found that students' attainment and behaviour were largely emotional responses to a teachers' behaviour and had powerful consequences. It is therefore important that teachers create supportive and non-threatening classroom environments for their students. In addition, a pupil's behaviour determined the teacher-pupil relationship. It was good if pupils were, responsive, enthusiastic and gave something back otherwise teachers refused to help, or make an investment or effort. Interestingly enough, both teachers and students alike expressed a strong need to feel cared for. It is important that students understand that their relationships with teachers involves the fulfilment of the needs of both parties and that teachers find it difficult to care about students who do not express positive behaviours towards them.

Similar to what the participants in this study suggested, Boles (2006) recommends that teachers familiarise themselves with other cultures so they can adequately support a multi-cultural set of pupils. For example, teachers may realise that what they consider misbehaving, is not considered as such in another culture and if they deal with it appropriately this will eliminate frustration and create a welcoming classroom atmosphere. Freire (2017) recommends recruitment of culturally relevant teachers, specifically Black teachers and support the development of cultural competencies among staff through cultural awareness training. White teachers can support this by acknowledging Black pupils' home languages in relationship to the English language as an example. In addition, they can ensure that the syllabus created reflects the full range of human existence, including Black culture. Ladson-Billings (2000) calls this situated pedagogy which can be helpful for teachers when they try to build relationships with Black pupils.

Limitations

Given the sensitive nature of this topic, it was difficult to recruit White teachers and as a result selection bias was one the study's limitations. In addition, the former Black pupils who decided to participate might have had different experiences from those who did not participate. What is more, the participants explored events that they might have experienced over ten years ago. Given the retrospective nature of data collection, there were limitations in the recollection of these memories. Also, the data richness came from the interviews and notes but data could have been even richer with a mixed methods of data collection including interviews, notes and surveys. Something else was the spacing of the interviews, which might have led to the forum not attracting as much participation because of the timing and the way it was set up might not have been conducive to interactive conversations. With some of the interviews, participants chose not to conduct them face-to-face, so they took place over the telephone. This suggests the various levels of comfort with participating in this kind of study. However, telephone interviews are limited in picking up non-verbal cues and restrict personal connections. The area pupils lived in was not explored as deeply, though a few participants discussed the socioeconomic stories from where they lived. In addition, the type of school, whether it was independent or state-run, determined the pupil's experiences and outcomes, so I could have explored this further. The participants in this study co-constructed narratives across multiple time points, but member checking was not used as a method to increase rigour and trustworthiness of the data. When we take into account the isolation, marginalisation and discrimination experienced by Black people, engaging participants in a more transformational process of shaping the telling of their stories would have been powerful. Given the diverse experiences of the participants, their social-economic status, privileges and oppressions interact in a complex and dynamic manner that was not fully captured in this study. The underlying issues of the intersections of race, class, gender, immigration status and religion could have been further developed to understand the layers of intersectional oppressions and privileges experienced by the participants. There was a shortage of studies on the experiences of Black pupils in England in the time frame and in some cases the study relied on literature from the United States.

Future Research

Future studies could explore the experiences of Black pupils in independent versus state schools. As well as the impact of the intersections of race and immigration on attainment. Another aspect that could be explored is the difference in schooling experience between the Black diasporic pupils and those that were partly educated in Africa or the Caribbean. I could have investigated the impact of the classroom size on the Black experience in school, including the impact on performance, behaviour, teacher-pupil interactions and pupil-pupil interactions. Also, more work needs to be done in the area of pupil choice of seat selection versus teacher's choice because the latter could be ethically appropriate and the former instrumental in classroom management. Finally, I could have explored the relationship between the culture of the city where the pupil lived and went to school and the culture of the parents' place of origin.

Implications for the Department for Education

The DfE may need to consider a global curriculum. One that is diverse, inclusive and representative of the communities and societies in England today. Just as the participants highlighted that they would have liked to learn about Africa and Asia and not just Europe and the Americas. As shown under the literature section, history, geography and English could incorporate the contributions of people of African descent to England and the developed world. African history and geography could be included in the curriculum from KS1 and could be an option for selection at KS3 or KS4. Finally, there could be a review into streaming or setting, as the majority of participants explained how this was detrimental to their schooling experience and academic performance. Instead, they should have mixed ability groups that promote peer support and collaboration.

Implications for Local Authorities

The local authorities should review budgets to ensure they invest in children and youth services including youth clubs. This will help alleviate some of the financial and related mental and social issues in the Black communities and children. Local authorities and schools should record, monitor and review incidents of racial discrimination and abuse. These should be tackled immediately because no child feels safe in an environment where racism occurs. If racist incidents occur unchallenged, then we are telling teachers, administrators, parents, support staff and children that racism is acceptable in society at large. Local authorities should set up departments to deal with racial discrimination issues that are led and run by people with lived experiences.

Implications for Educators and Administrators

As schools create opportunities to celebrate diversity based on racial, ethnic and cultural backgrounds especially during Black history month, they could consider including this in the budgets and calendar throughout the school year. School staff and administrative bodies should be representative and diverse. One participant pointed out that they did not think they would have completed their course in college had it not been for the arrival of a Black teacher to their school. In addition, other participants indicated the difference a Black teacher made to their schooling experience and lives. As identified in this study, teachers play a role in the lives of pupils. Being able to access teachers during out of school hours could be particularly important for relationship building or getting help with school tasks. Schools could increase school hours to provide breakfast and dinner where possible to pupils. School staff and administrators could create opportunities to embrace cultural diversity, such as creating workshops, panels and classes on Black culture and they could get involved in the local communities that they teach in. Another idea could be to invite Black professionals who specialise in inclusion and diversity to train school staff and administrators. Schools could use available data to analyse attainment levels by ethnicity in order to know how best to support students. However, It is important to avoid categorisations such as Black, Asian and Minority Ethnic because the school experiences of the individuals deemed to belong to these groups are not monolithic. All literacy and literature materials could have positive African characters and illustrations so that Black pupils can relate to them. School libraries could stock books by Black authors which could be used in the classroom on a daily basis. Schools should have a clear stand on racism with unambiguous policies including recruitment. Finally, schools could support parents whose first language is not English. They could setup workshops that help the parents understand how best to support their children. Just as this study demonstrated that some Black parents who experienced schooling in a different country did not have a full understanding of the English education system.

Implications for Parents

The English curriculum as highlighted by this research does not teach Black pupils about their history or reflect Black people in a positive way. Therefore, Black parents may need to take it upon themselves to educate Black children about their history, the geography of Africa and incorporate culturally appropriate reading materials. Similar to one participant who explained that they take their son back to the Caribbean during the school holidays and it is during this time that their son is educated on his history. Another option could be attending Black Saturday schools, or workshops run by the Black community. In addition, parents, especially those who were not educated in England, could do some research about the experiences of Black pupils in the English education system so they can prepare their children for school. Preparation should start from day one: when one arrives into the country. For the Black children born in England, preparation should start when the baby is born. Parents could look at prospective schools to find out how many Black teaching and non-teaching staff a school has: the number of Black pupils in a school: the school's policy on dealing with racism and discrimination: exclusion rates: and behavioural policy. This might give them an idea of how diverse and inclusive a school is. Parents could take an interest in the children's school work and ensure they know what level their child is performing at. This will help the parent determine what level of support they can offer the child. Parents can get this support for their children from private education providers, the school or they can teach the children themselves.

Lessons Learned

Narrative inquiry calls for a prolonged engagement with the storytellers and time to soak up their stories. Therefore, timeliness and planning were very important. As with any research, dealing with rich data piece by piece was necessary to stop the feeling of being overwhelmed and drowning in one's data. In future qualitative projects, I hope to remain engaged with the data more consistently. In addition, I learned about the relevance of the writing process in qualitative work. The notes I wrote during the interview process were very helpful in the analysis. In the process of writing, my ideas flowed and developed, binding with the participants stories. My notes were not that different from their storytelling. I had the honour of meeting these former pupils and teachers and being able to hear their stories, some of which were emotional. This has helped me learn about how, within context, all stories make sense. When society does not celebrate us, it leads to a world of hidden stories that extends a feeling of disconnection, when really, the missing pieces may be silenced. In finding these pieces, I better understood how holistically consistent and connected the participants were and how their stories were tools for empowerment, healing and social change.

Conclusion

This study examined how the English national curriculum between the 1950's and 2000 and teacher pedagogical approach impacted the academic performance of Black pupils. Through the lens of narrative therapy, I hoped to generate rich narratives of the participants' experiences. Poor academic performance and schooling experience of Black pupils is a continuing trend in England. Thus, I hope that others will read the stories in this book, learn from and relate to the participant's struggles, courage and resilience. All pupils deserve to have a quality education, one that prepares them for a successful future, so that they are able to retire in dignity. For Black pupils to feel like school is for them too, they should be taught a global curriculum: in mixed ability groups: with high teacher expectations. It could be an urban pedagogical approach: a mixture of teacher and pupil-led style of teaching: in medium classes of between 15-20. The seating arrangement could be at round tables or hot-desking with a regular rotation plan arranged by the pupils. Finally, the government could invest in and incentivise teacher training courses to recruit Black student teachers. Schools could also do their part in ensuring the recruitment and support of Black teaching and non-teaching staff as well as administrators (see figure 5, for a new framework that would promote success for Black pupils in education).

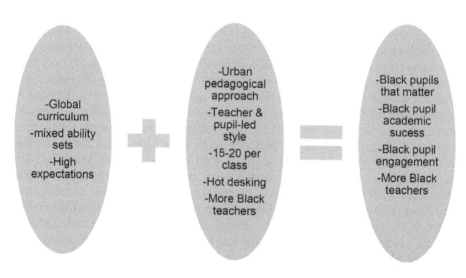

Figure 5
A Global curriculum and Urban pedagogical approach

Index

Black students: 21, 36, 40, 43, 46, 47, 51, 64, 76
Black teachers: 45, 70, 87,103
Boles: 98, 103
Bologna: 3
bottom: 29, 37, 39, 44, 46, 51, 54, 60, 62, 71, 76, 80, 85
bottom sets: 29, 39, 44, 46, 51, 58, 62, 71,76, 78, 80, 85
boys: 1, 3, 20, 30, 42, 70, 85, 102
Bristol: 93, 96
Britain: 39, 54, 83, 84, 93, 95, 97
Britain's role in slavery: 83
British imperialism: 57
bullies: 102

C
Cambridge: 32, 43
celebrate: 50, 72, 74, 105, 107
change: 3, 9, 38, 39, 42, 49, 52, 53 62, 64, 66, 67, 69, 72, 79, 92, 107
child: 5-7, 10, 29, 30, 39, 42, 44, 46, 47
China: 96
churches: 2, 3
class: 1, 2, 6, 17, 30, 31, 32, 33, 34, 36, 39, 40, 42, 43, 44, 45, 46, 47, 50,
51, 52, 55, 57,58, 60, 61, 62, 63, 65,66, 67, 68, 69, 70, 71, 72, 73, 74
classroom: 8, 9, 16, 20, 26, 28, 30, 32, 34, 36, 37, 38, 40, 43, 44, 45,
47, 52, 55, 56, 58, 61, 63, 70, 71, 73
Classroom Set-up: 26, 30, 32, 34, 36, 38, 40, 43, 45, 47, 52, 55, 58,
61, 64, 66, 67, 70, 71, 73, 76, 78, 80, 88, 101
Classroom Size: 30, 32, 34, 36, 37, 40, 43, 44, 47, 52, 55, 58, 61, 63,
66, 67, 70, 71, 73, 76, 78, 88, 101, 105
colleges: 3, 4, 6, 15
confidence: 50, 51, 57, 62, 77, 84, 90, 99, 101
confident: 37, 38, 51, 55, 62, 73, 86
conversation: 22, 41, 55, 104
core subjects: 4, 16, 28, 37, 39, 57, 63, 65, 76, 85
country: 37, 38, 39, 57, 58, 60, 61, 62, 63, 65, 69, 80, 83, 86, 95, 100, 106
cultural awareness training: 41, 43
cultures: 50, 63, 72, 75, 98, 103
curriculum: 3, 4, 5, 6, 10, 11, 12, 13, 14, 16, 22, 25, 26, 29, 36, 39 40,
42, 44, 46, 48, 50, 53

D
DfE (Department for Education): 11, 105
Diane Abbott: 95
disability: 7, 10, 29, 85
Disability: 7
discrimination: 5, 7, 67, 104, 105, 107
dyslexia: 29, 85

E

F

G

LEA (local education authority): 5, 6
learning: 1, 7–9, 12, 17, 20, 29, 30–32, 33, 39, 40, 41, 42, 43
lessons, 25–26, 28–29, 33, 38–40, 44–46, 49, 51–52, 54, 56–57, 59, 61–63
levels: 10, 13, 18, 29, 31, 42, 57, 58, 62, 65, 69, 70, 72, 85, 98,
99, 104, 106
life: 7, 10, 12, 14, 16, 21, 22, 23, 32, 37, 38, 41
listening: 14, 30, 87
literature: 11, 17, 19, 42, 54, 93, 95, 97, 98, 104, 105
lived experiences: 1, 13, 19, 20, 21, 105
Liverpool: 96–97
London: 15, 23, 40, 72, 93, 94, 95–97
love: 29, 30, 32, 48, 60, 63, 75, 78, 80, 85, 91
lower set: 29, 33, 39, 46, 54, 62, 27, 76, 78
low expectations: 29, 60, 76, 86

M
Mary Seacole: 94
maths: 31–33, 36–38, 42, 44, 49–49
Members of Parliament (MPs): 95
middle: 1, 3, 5, 11, 30, 33, 34, 37, 38, 46, 49, 50
middle sets: 50, 60, 62, 67
mixed groups: 51, 72, 85
Multicultural Literature: 103
mum: 44, 46, 47, 48, 50, 60, 61, 64, 65, 70, 91

N
narrative accounts: 12, 15, 19, 21, 28
National Council for Vocational Qualifications (NCVQ): 6
national curriculum: 4, 6, 10, 11, 12, 13, 15, 25, 39
National Curriculum Council (NCC): 6
Negro: 15
notes: 18, 19, 20, 21, 33, 34, 93, 104, 107
numbers: 2, 17, 30, 32, 64, 89, 93

O
Organisation of Women of African and Asian Descent (OWAAD: 95
Ottobah Cugoano: 93
Ottoman Empire: 2

P
parents:5, 7, 10, 11, 15, 16, 20, 28, 31, 39, 40, 43–46,
53, 57, 58, 60, 61
Paris: 3
parishes: 2
Parliament: 3, 5, 95, 96
participants: 11, 13–16, 20, 21–28, 82–90
pedagogical approach: 10–13, 18, 79, 87, 107, 108

pedagogy: 8–12, 14, 16, 17, 22, 26, 27, 30, 32, 38, 41, 43, 52, 53, 56, 64, 66, 75, 82

peers: 28, 33, 42, 54, 57, 89, 99, 101

performance: 1, 4, 7, 10, 11, 13, 16, 17 22, 30, 31, 32, 34, 36, 37, 38, 40

physics: 31–33, 55, 87

physics lessons: 32, 89

planters: 93, 96

police: 30, 90

Pope Pius IV: 3

power: 7–9, 22, 23, 101

pre-planned sitting arrangement: 52, 67, 76, 89, 102

President Obama: 69, 70

pressure: 33, 34, 53, 54, 66, 89

primary school: 6, 15, 42, 43, 46, 48, 50, 51

problems: 9, 30, 46, 52, 55, 57, 61, 88

Q

QCA (Qualifications and Curriculum Authority), 6

Qualifications and Curriculum Authority (QCA), 6

Qur'an, 2

R

race: 5, 7, 38, 42, 48, 55, 62, 64, 65, 74, 76

racism: 17, 36, 69, 78, 85, 94, 98, 100, 105–107

racist: 43, 59, 60, 69, 71, 88, 105

relationship: 1, 4, 7, 8, 14, 20, 22, 23, 26, 28, 30, 32, 34, 36, 38, 41, 43

Relationship and Sex Education (RSE): 7

religions: 1, 7, 54, 65, 76, 83, 104

Representation: 12, 25, 28, 29, 31, 33, 36, 37, 39, 42

researcher-participant relationships: 20

rights5, 7, 15, 16, 24, 46, 57, 95

royal family: 50

Rwanda: 65, 84

S

SCAA (School Curriculum and Assessment Authority): 6

School Examinations and Assessment Council (SEAC): 6

school hours: 68, 90, 106

schools: 1–8, 10–12, 16, 22, 23, 40, 43–46

sciences: 32, 39, 57, 59, 78, 90

secondary school: 5, 15, 43, 46, 48, 51, 53, 59, 62, 65, 72, 75, 85, 91, 99

SEN (special educational needs;>): 6, 7, 10, 46, 73, 85, 89

SENCO: 62

sets: 1, 4, 5, 11, 16, 62, 65, 67

situated pedagogies: 101, 103

V
values: 1, 14, 22, 23, 43, 50, 58, 82, 83, 98
vocal: 46, 47, 91
voices: 12, 18, 19, 83

W
West Indian: 58, 95
White: 11, 15, 17, 22
White pupils: 17, 36, 46, 52
White teachers: 11, 17, 22, 34, 42, 46, 53, 103
Windrush: 94
world: 1, 3, 4, 8, 33, 44, 54, 60, 62
world's top slave trader: 95

Y
year: 4, 5, 10, 13, 14, 16, 17, 20

Z
Zanzibar: 95

References

Bamberg, M. (2010) 'Narrative Analysis', APA handbook of research methods in psychology, 2, pp. 77-94.

Bicard, D.F., Ervin, A., Bicard, S.C. and Baylot-Casey., L. (2012) 'DIFFERENTIAL EFFECTS OF SITTING ARRANGEMENTS ON DISRUPTIVE BEHAVIOR OF FIFTH GRADE STUDENTS DURING INDEPENDENT SITWORK', Journal of applied behaviour analysis, 45(2), pp. 407-411. doi: 10.1901/jaba.2012.45-407.

Blanden, J. and Gregg, P. (2004) Family Income and Educational Attainment: A Review of Approaches and Evidence for Britain. Centre for the Economics of Education, London School of Economics and Political Science.

Boles, M. (2006a) The Effects of Multicultural Literature in the Classroom. DigitalCommons@EMU.

Boles, M. (2006b) The Effects of Multicultural Literature in the Classroom. DigitalCommons@EMU.

Burgess, S.M. and Greaves, E. (2013) 'Test scores, subjective assessment, and stereotyping of ethnic minorities', Journal of labor economics, 31(3), pp. 535-576. doi: 10.1086/669340.

Chowdry, H., Crawford, C., Dearden, L., Goodman, A. and Vignoles, A. (2013) 'Widening Participation in Higher Education: Analysis Using linked Administrative Data', Journal of the Royal Statistical Society. Series A, Statistics in society, 176(2), pp. 431-457. doi: 10.1111/j.1467-985X.2012.01043. x.

Clandinin, D., J and Connelly, F., M (2000a) Narrative inquiry. 1. ed. edn. San Francisco: Jossey-Bass.

Clandinin, D.J. and Connelly, F.M. (2000b) Narrative inquiry. 1. ed. edn. San Francisco: Jossey-Bass.

Coard, B. (1971) How the West Indian child is made educationally subnormal in the British school system. London: New Beacon Books. Cooper, K. and Stewart, K. (2013) Does money affect children's outcomes?: a systematic review. York: Joseph Rowntree Foundation. Available at: (Accessed: 01/10/2021).

Creswell, J., W (2013) Qualitative inquiry & research design. Third edition edn. Los Angeles: London: New Delhi: Singapore: Washington DC: SAGE.

Creswell, J., W and Poth, C., N (2018) Qualitative inquiry & research design. Fourth edition, international student edition edn. Los Angeles: London: New Delhi: Singapore: Washington DC: SAGE.

Demie, F. (2018) Black Caribbean Achievement in Schools in England. Available at: https://www.lambeth.gov.uk/rsu/sites/www.lambeth.gov.uk.rsu/file s/black_caribbean_achievement_executive_summary.pdf (Accessed: 10/10/2021).

Department for Education (2014) National curriculum in England: framework for key stages 1 to 4. London: DfE. Available at: https://www.gov.uk/government/publications/national-curriculum-in-england-framework-for-key-stages-1-to-4/the-national-curriculum-in-england-framework-for-key-stages-1-to-4 (Accessed: 14/09/21).

Department for Education (2011) Class Size and Education in England evidence report. Available at: https://assets.publishing.ser-vice.gov.uk/government/uploads/system/uploads/attachment_data/f ile/183364/DFE-RR169.pdf (Accessed: 11/10/2021).

Education Endowment Foundation (2021) Best Evidence on Impact of COVID-19 on Pupil Attainment. London: Education Endowment Foundation (EEF). Available at: https://educationendowmentfounda-tion.org.uk/covid-19-resources/best-evidence-on-impact-of-school-closures-on-the-attainment-gap/ (Accessed: 13/09/2021).

Education Endowment Foundation (2018) Closing the Attainment Gap. London: Education Endowment Foundation (EEF). Available at: https://educationendowmentfoundation.org.uk/evidence-sum-maries/attainment-gap/ (Accessed: 13/09/2021).

Education Endowment Foundation (2021) Setting and Streaming. Available at: https://educationendowmentfoundation.org.uk/educa-tion-evidence/teaching-learning-toolkit/setting-and-streaming#close-Signup (Accessed: 10/10/2021).

Finn, J., D and Achilles, C., M (1999) 'Tennessee's Class Size Study: Findings, Implications, Misconceptions', Educational evaluation and policy analysis, 21(2), pp. 97-109. doi: 10.3102/01623737021002097.

Freire, P. (2017) Pedagogy of the Oppressed. Britain: Penguin Classics.

Fryer, P. (2010) Staying power. New. ed edn. London [u.a.]: Pluto Pr.

Goldstein, H. and Blatchford, P. (1998) 'Class Size and Educational Achievement: a review of methodology with particular reference to study design', British educational research journal, 24(3), pp. 255-268. doi: 10.1080/0141192980240302.

Gonzalez, T.A. (1984) 'The Relationship of Teachers' Conceptions of Mathematics and Mathematics Teaching to Instructional Practice',

Educational studies in mathematics, 15(2), pp. 105-127. doi: 10.1007/BF00305892.

Haynes, J., Tikly, L. and Caballero, C. (2006) 'The barriers to achievement for White/Black Caribbean pupils in English schools', British journal of sociology of education, 27(5), pp. 569-583. doi: 10.1080/01425690600958766.

Illich, I. (1971) Deschooling Society. New York [u.a.]: Harper & Row.

Kim, J. (2015) Understanding Narrative Inquiry: The Crafting and Analysis of Stories as Research. Sage Publications.

Ladson-Billings, G. (2000) 'Fighting for Our Lives', Journal of teacher education, 51(3), pp. 206-214. doi: 10.1177/0022487100051003008. Lovejoy, P., E (1989) 'The Impact of the Atlantic Slave Trade on Africa: A Review of the Literature', Journal of African history, 11(3), pp. 45-28. doi: 10.1017/S0021853700024439.

Mac an Ghaill, M. (1988) Young, Gifted and Black. 1. publ. edn. Milton Keynes [u.a.]: Open Univ. Press.

Minchen, B.J. (2007) The Effects of Classroom Sitting on Students' Performance in a High School Science Setting. Available at: http://digitalcommons.brockport.edu/ehd_theses/414 (Accessed: 15/10/2021).

Murray, C. and Malmgren, K. (2005) 'Implementing a teacher–student relationship program in a high-poverty urban school: Effects on social, emotional, and academic adjustment and lessons learned', Journal of school psychology, 43(2), pp. 137-152. doi: 10.1016/j.jsp.2005.01.003.

Nelson, R.F., Irons, J.R., Latty, R.S., Williams, D.L., Toll, D.L., Markham, B.L. and Stauffer, M.L. (1984) Impact of Thematic Mapper Sensor Characteristics on Classification Accuracy. Available at: http://ntrs.nasa.gov/search.jsp?R=19840022341 (Accessed: 20/10/2021).

Ollerenshaw, J., A and Creswell, J., W (2002) 'Narrative Research: A Comparison of Two Restorying Data Analysis Approaches', Qualitative inquiry, 8(3), pp. 329-347. doi: 10.1177/10778004008003008.

Olusoga, D. (2016) Black and British. London: Macmillan.

Organisation for Economic Co-operation and Development (2018) Equity in education: breaking down barriers to social mobility. OECD Publishing. Available at: https://search.informit.org/documentSummary:res=APO:dn=201966 (Accessed: 11/10/2021).

Patton, M., Q (2002) Qualitative research & evaluation methods. 3. ed. edn. Thousand Oaks [u.a.]: Sage.

Perry, J. (1971) 'Black Literature and the English Curriculum', English journal, 60(8), pp. 1057-1062. doi: 10.2307/814027.

Pillas, D., Marmot, M., Naicker, K., Goldblatt, P., Morrison, J. and Pikhart, H. (2014) 'Social inequalities in early childhood health and development: a European-wide systematic review', Pediatric research, 76(5), pp. 418-424. doi: 10.1038/pr.2014.122.

Pinnegar, S. and Daynes, J., G (2007) 'Locating Narrative Inquiry Historically: Thematics in the Turn to Narrative'Handbook of Narrative Inquiry: Mapping a Methodology Thousand Oaks: SAGE Publications, Inc, pp. 3.

Pumfrey, P.D. (1990) Race Relations and Urban Education. 1. publ. edn. London u.a: Falmer.

Riessman, C., K (2008) Narrative methods for the human sciences. Los Angeles: London: New Delhi: Singapore: SAGE Publications.

Rodney, W. (1974) How Europe underdeveloped Africa. Washington, DC: Howard Univ. Press.

Russell, R., C (1960) History of Elementary Schools & Adult Education in Nettleton and Caistor.

Saunders, M., Lewis, P. and Thornhill, A. (2016) Research methods for business students. 7th ed. edn. Harlow, England: Pearson.

Wiesner-Hanks, M., E (2013) Early Modern Europe. 2. ed. edn. Cambridge [u.a.]: Cambridge Univ. Press.

Wilkins, J. (2014) 'Good Teacher-Student Relationships: Perspectives of Teachers in Urban High Schools', American secondary education, 43(1), pp. 52-68.

Wright, C. (1986) Education for Some: The Educational and Vocational Experiences of 15–18-Year-Old Members of Minority and Ethnic Groups, Stoke-on-Trent: Trentham Books.

Other Books by Wasuk Godwin Sule-Pearce

Titles	ISBN
The Geography of East Africa **Study** Book	978-1-7399980-0-4
The Geography of East Africa **Activity** Book	978-1-7399980-1-1
The Geography of West Africa **Study** Book	978-1-7399980-2-8
The Geography of West Africa **Activity** Book	978-1-7399980-3-5
The Geography of Central Africa **Study** Book	978-1-7399980-4-2
The Geography of Central Africa **Activity** Book	978-1-7399980-5-9
The Geography of Southern Africa **Study** Book	978-1-7399980-6-6
The Geography of Southern Africa **Activity** Book	978-1-7399980-7-3
The Geography of The Horn of Africa **Study** Book	978-1-7399980-8-0
The Geography of The Horn of Africa **Activity** Book	978-1-7399980-9-7

Also available as a set:
The Geography of Africa
Pack of 10 **Study** & **Activity** Books   978-1-3999-1187-0

For more information about the above titles, please visit:
https://wasukp.com/

Coming soon

Titles

The History of East Africa **Study** Book
The History of East Africa **Activity** Book
The History of West Africa **Study** Book
The History of West Africa **Activity** Book
The History of Central Africa **Study** Book
The History of Central Africa **Activity** Book
The History of Southern Africa **Study** Book
The History of Southern Africa **Activity** Book
The History of The Horn of Africa **Study** Book
The History of The Horn of Africa **Activity** Book

Also available as a set:
The History of Africa
Pack of 10 **Study** & **Activity** Books

Lightning Source UK Ltd.
Milton Keynes UK
UKHW031549100222
398491UK00006B/296